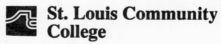

TALKING POLITICS

TALKING POLITICS

Choosing the President in the Television Age

LIZ CUNNINGHAM

PRAEGER

Westport, Connecticut
London

Library of Congress Cataloging-in-Publication Data

Cunningham, Liz.
    Talking politics : choosing the president in the television
age / Liz Cunningham.
        p. cm.
    Includes bibliographical references and index.
    ISBN 0–275–94187–6 (alk. paper)
    1. Television news anchors—United States—Interviews.
2. Television and politics—United States. 3. United States—
Politics and government—1981– 4. United States—Politics and
government—1981–1989. I. Title.
PN4871.C86   1995
791.45′028′092273—dc20   94–21694

British Library Cataloguing in Publication Data is available.

Library of Congress Catalog Card Number: 94–21694
ISBN: 0–275–94187–6

First published in 1995

Praeger Publishers, 88 Post Road West, Westport, CT 06881
An imprint of Greenwood Publishing Group, Inc.

Printed in the United States of America

The paper used in this book complies with the
Permanent Paper Standard issued by the National
Information Standards Organization (Z39.48–1984).

10 9 8 7 6 5 4 3 2 1

to Vivian

CONTENTS

Acknowledgments   ix

Introduction   xi

1   Robert MacNeil   1

2   Linda Ellerbee   21

3   Larry King   35

4   Pierre Salinger   49

5   Dave Sirulnick   65

6   Jeff Greenfield   83

7   Geraldine Ferraro   95

8   Bernard Shaw   111

9   Tom Brokaw   127

10   Roger Rosenblatt   143

Epilogue   155

Bibliography   163

Index   165

ACKNOWLEDGMENTS

Books are often ensemble creations, this one especially so. I am very thankful to each contributor, Tom Brokaw, Linda Ellerbee, Geraldine Ferraro, Jeff Greenfield, Larry King, Robert MacNeil, Roger Rosenblatt, Pierre Salinger, Dave Sirulnick, and Bernard Shaw, for taking the time for extended interviews, some over the course of several years.

I am greatly indebted to friends and colleagues for their encouragement, support, and advice. For this I am especially thankful to Barbara Baker, Bruce Baker, Bob Brown, Cynthia Brown, Katherine Ball, Sarah Busing, Richard Catalano, Charles Cavaliere, Dana Davis, Barbara Freeman, Mary Glenn, Dorian Gossy, Linda Hall, Holly Hartley, Claude Heckscher, Jan Johnson, Steven Katona, Catherine Keller, Susan Lerner, Margaret Livingston, Peter Miller, Karen Narita, Jack Phillips, Louis Rabineau, Janet Reed, Alan Ross, Merl Ross, Cathy Shin, Monica Stroscher, Sheri Tibbles, and Michael Waldman.

To my assistant, Deborah Tillman, my heartfelt thanks for her excellent research and insightful commentary. And to Paul Dickson I owe a great debt of gratitude for his savvy counsel. I am very thankful to my editors at Praeger, James Dunton, Catherine Lyons, Margaret Maybury, Denise Van Acker, and Susan Thornton, for their fine work.

To my agent, Bill Alder, Jr., who came in at the eleventh hour and turned the clock back, I cannot express enough appreciation. And I'm very grateful to Beth Pratt-Dewey and Lisa Swain for their help, especially their split-second brainstorming smarts. I will always be thankful to Edward Meade, Jr. for his endless encouragement and good humor. Last, my heartfelt thanks to Carol Gibbon and Vivian Hankin, who I am honored to know and whose support made all the difference.

INTRODUCTION

Every presidential campaign, television journalists and politicians race through months of picnics and press conferences, tractor rides and talk shows until Election Day. It's a race of monumental proportions—the all-powerful television and television journalism locked in tandem with the quest for the American presidency, the world's seat of power. The sheer volume of airtime, equipment, and personnel is staggering. The campaign for the presidency can be profound and historic; it can also be comic, clumsy, and demeaning and degenerate into a mean-spirited media circus, a jumble of murky revelations and brass-knuckled attacks.

Throughout it all broadcasters and candidates are tied together. However much they admire, respect, fascinate, detest, fear, or resent each other, by and large they must go left foot, right foot, to the finish. If things go well, they are first-name chums: "Larry," "Robin," and "Tom." If things sour, they can be archenemies. But whether they are anxious friends or intimate enemies, their relationship shapes the words and images by which most Americans choose their president.

This book is about that relationship between broadcasters and presidential candidates. In 1988, while preparing an article on presidential campaigns, I began interviewing journalists and politicians about the role of the media. I was especially struck by the ferocity of many of these conversations. To the people I interviewed, the role of the media has everything to do with how we as Americans think and feel and know our world—it is the primary lens through which we choose our president, a choice which is nothing less than a turning point in history. It was a subject that was as personal as it was serious, one that brought to a head their sense of right and wrong in politics, and their hopes, disappointments, and anxieties about the nation's welfare. It was then that I decided to assemble a book through which a reader could "listen in" on these conversations, a series of interviews that would reflect the experiences and personality of each person I spoke with.

That decision led me to interview some of the most interesting and controversial broadcasters, journalists, and political commentators who have been involved in presidential campaigns—NBC anchor Tom Brokaw, offbeat and ever-candid broadcast journalist Linda Ellerbee, vice-presidential candidate Geraldine Ferraro, media critic and political analyst for ABC News' *Nightline* Jeff Greenfield, CNN talk-show host Larry King, *The MacNeil/Lehrer NewsHour*'s Robert MacNeil, essayist and author Roger Rosenblatt, former press secretary to John F. Kennedy and ABC News correspondent and bureau chief Pierre Salinger, CNN anchor Bernard Shaw, and MTV News director Dave Sirulnick.

Through the eyes of these individuals, this book is a window into the world that shapes what we see on television during presidential campaigns and how we choose and judge our candidates. Oral-history interviews have an unusual capacity to reveal how individuals think and how they make decisions through stories and jokes, arguments and beliefs. You will find stories of relentless and sometimes explosive interviews, of smear campaigns, death threats, broken promises and situations in which journalists found themselves unwittingly manipulated.

Like lodestones certain issues and events surface again and again in the interviews—fairness and bias, sensationalism, elitism, privacy, polls, ratings, talk shows, Ronald Reagan's Teflon veneer, Michael Dukakis's unemotional demeanor, and of course, the persistent and extraordinary impact of John F. Kennedy's presidency. Of all of these "lodestones," one in particular surfaced most, like some ineluctable magnet—the issue of character. In America, a nation that lacks religious unity and has no monarchy, the character of the president is tremendously important. And despite all the distortion, manipulation, political huckstering, and outright lies, television and television journalists have given us a unique window on it.

Especially during presidential campaigns, voters perform an acutely modern form of emotional reconnaissance, sizing up a candidate on the screen, searching for some flicker of recognition, a feeling for the candidate. We are listening and looking for someone to fill the role of president, a person who can lead us into the future, whose character can give definition to an era. That process of sizing-up candidates is returned to again and again in these discussions.

As candidates choose to appear more and more on talk shows and in electronic town meetings, and as unconventional news divisions such as MTV News flourish, the media environment surrounding presidential campaigns will continue to change. But the issues which concern television journalism and presidential candidates, such as fairness and bias, distortion and manipulation, will persist in new forms. And we will still be asking of the candidate, "Who is this person, really?" And the candidate will still face the wide-eyed gaze of the camera. There will still be questions and answers, quips and attacks, flashes of warmth and aloofness—all funneled through that persistent, beguiling synergy among the candidate, the images, and reality.

TALKING POLITICS

1

ROBERT MACNEIL

Robert MacNeil is Executive Editor and Co-Anchor of
The MacNeil/Lehrer NewsHour.

One evening in 1966 Robert MacNeil and his wife called
on Richard Nixon at his New York City apartment. An
interview had been arranged as part of MacNeil's coverage
of Nixon for NBC and MacNeil had asked his wife, Jane,
to join him so that they could compare impressions afterward.

Both were well aware of Nixon's "press as enemy" attitude. After Nixon lost the 1962 gubernatorial race in
California, he'd sniped at a group of journalists that they
wouldn't have "Nixon to kick around anymore." But now
Nixon was carefully positioning himself for the 1968 presidential election and trying to start fresh. MacNeil interviewed a "new" Nixon that evening. Nixon was friendlier,
more gracious.

MacNeil and his wife rode up to Nixon's apartment in a
wood-paneled elevator. A Filipino butler, dressed in a
white jacket, led them to a study where Nixon greeted
them. Nixon cheerfully expressed his dismay that "Pat
and the girls" weren't able to meet them. MacNeil later
recalled that his wife "was sure they were there."[1]

Five years later MacNeil would be working for the National Public Affairs Center for Television (NPACT), the public television precursor to PBS. Nixon's staff would wage a smear campaign to defame MacNeil as part of a bureaucratic war with public television. White House memos would refer to those "left-wing commentators who are cutting us up"[2] and MacNeil would deliver a scathing speech accusing Nixon appointees of "perverting" the goals of journalism.[3] Two years after, in 1973, MacNeil and his partner, Jim Lehrer, would launch the gavel-to-gavel coverage of the Watergate hearings that kept Americans glued to their television sets as the Byzantine maze of the Watergate scandal came unraveled.

But that evening in his study in 1966, Nixon surprised his guests with unexpected charm. He asked Jane Mac-Neil about her pregnancy and about Washington, her hometown. When they settled down to the interview Mac-Neil's questions were no-nonsense and Nixon's answers were straightforward, displaying his meticulous grasp of the political scene. However startled MacNeil was at the disappearance of Nixon's dark side, his tendency to be reclusive and sometimes vengeful, neither of them would have predicted what the future would bring.

Several days later MacNeil watched Nixon give an interview from the control room of a television station. Nixon's face appeared on an array of black-and-white and color monitors. "Suddenly it struck me," recalls MacNeil, "that I was watching two different men. The black-and-white monitors brought out the dark Nixon . . . color made him far more personable and cheerful a character."[4] The 1960 campaign between Kennedy and Nixon was one of the closest in history. "Had a mere delay in introducing color television cost Nixon the presidency in 1960?" Mac-Neil mused. "Considering his narrow win over Hubert

Humphrey, did color television give him the White House in 1968?"5

That moment in the control room was one of many which fueled MacNeil's fascination with the intermixing of politics and television. MacNeil began his career as a television journalist just as television began to influence politics significantly, and he has been both a practitioner and an unrestrained critic of television journalism ever since. The Canadian-born MacNeil began his career in 1955 at the Reuters News Agency in London. He signed on with NBC News as a roving correspondent in 1960, and in 1965 became the New York anchor for NBC's *Scherer-MacNeil Report*. During his tenure at NBC he covered some of the most dramatic moments of the early sixties, including the Cuban Missile Crisis, the building of the Berlin Wall, and the assassination of John Kennedy. In 1967 he returned to London as a reporter for the British Broadcasting Corporation.

As he covered the events of the sixties, MacNeil became more and more frustrated with what he saw as the distortion of events by television news. In 1968, he put his thoughts together in his first book, *The People Machines: The Influence of Television on American Politics*, which deeply criticized the tactics used by television newscasts to attract audiences and the manipulation of the media by politicians. In 1971, MacNeil left the BBC to become a senior correspondent for NPACT, and in 1973, he teamed up with Jim Lehrer for the first time when they co-anchored the Senate Watergate Hearings.

MacNeil and Lehrer shared similar frustrations with the style of network news reporting and a strong desire to report the news in a less commercial format. In 1975 they launched the first nightly PBS newscast, which featured a half-hour report devoted to in-depth coverage of a single issue. Originally called *The Robert MacNeil Report with*

Jim Lehrer, the newscast was a dream come true for MacNeil and Lehrer. They could act as their own editors, free of the commercial pressures faced by the major networks. In 1983 the broadcast was expanded to a full hour of news and became *The MacNeil / Lehrer NewsHour*. Since the beginning their coverage has distinguished itself for its innovative in-depth coverage of issues. Indeed, many have observed that recently network newscasts have become "MacNeil/Lehrer–ized," giving more emphasis to issues and "talking-heads" discussions.

During presidential campaigns the *NewsHour*'s coverage of photo-ops and staged events is kept to a minimum, and stump speeches are often broadcast in full. In 1992 the *NewsHour* joined forces with NBC News to cover the Democratic and Republican conventions jointly. Their joint coverage drew widespread acclaim for combining the best of both worlds, extensive NBC convention coverage and the *NewsHour*'s in-depth commentary and analysis.

While MacNeil is now very much in his element at the *NewsHour*, he is still eager to talk about the media and politics and has participated as host, narrator, and producer of numerous public television productions, including the nine-part series *The Story of English*, for which he co-authored the companion book. He has also authored numerous books since *The People Machines*, including *The Right Place at the Right Time*, which chronicles his experiences as a journalist; *Wordstruck*, a memoir about his fascination with the English language; and most recently, his first novel, *The Burden of Desire*.

Among other issues, MacNeil discusses in this interview the explosive Bush-Rather exchange in 1988 during a live *CBS Nightly News* interview. Bush had taunted Rather about Rather's walking off the set of a broadcast, because the CBS newscast was being held up by a tennis match. Rather and Bush exchanged jabs in what resembled a

verbal prizefight—Bush attempting to put "the wimp factor" which plagued him to rest, and Rather trying to nail
Bush down on the Iran-contra scandal. The heated exchange was a moment when the tensions between candidate and journalist boiled to the surface.

*What do you think happened when Dan Rather and
George Bush fought on the air in 1988?*

Well, I think it was a sort of marvelous symbol of a number
of things. On the straight journalistic level, Bush had
dodged questions about his role in Iran-contra. It was very
legitimate to try and get him on the record about that. It's
highly unusual for *CBS Evening News* to do an interview
live in their news show, because it's uncontrollable. The
Bush people could predict what the area of questioning
would be. And so if Rather was going to booby-trap them,
then they were going to booby-trap him—and somebody
fed Bush this line. It's all been documented, who gave him
the line and everything, to taunt Rather and put him off
his stroke—about his walking out on the program.

Now, what made it interesting to me, as somebody who
interviews people live on the program, and is used to
it—there is a great deal of anxiety in a television program
about the way the time is passing. On our program a
nine-minute interview is nothing, we do them all the time,
sometimes half-hour interviews. On a nightly news program, nobody can be used to that. It's so highly unusual
and the minutes are so valuable that you're bound to be
impatient to extract from the interviewee everything that
you can drag out of him as fast as possible. Because the
clock is ticking: it's a clock ticking more loudly than any
clock ticks in anybody's mind except maybe for the few
seconds before somebody's executed.

So, psychologically, the pressure on Rather, in that
unusual situation, to extract something good from Bush
quickly would be greater than it would be for Koppel or for

us, who are used to doing extended interviews. There is a further professional observation. Rather and the other people who've been on *60 Minutes* are used to the extended taped interview, which may last an hour or an hour and a half, which they then edit. The network has an expectation of success in such an interview that you "get the goodies." It may take an hour and a half to get them—but, it's like any journalist interviewing, you interview and you interview and then you hear the nugget that you want and you put that nugget on the air.

It's hard to resist the expectation that you can do that in the live interview, and that it's a kind of proof of your machismo and your skill as a television reporter that you can duplicate that kind of editorial efficiency in the live situation, which you can't. It's hard to conceive of a person in Dan Rather's situation—with the network having made its reputation with *60 Minutes* and the nightly news, on the ability to "get the goodies"—not to feel an enormous impatience to get that kind of efficiency. That's why he appeared to be jumping down Bush's throat. . . . He would have been thinking to himself, I assume, "God, we've got to get this stuff out of him!" The whole culture of the network expectations and the politician's expectations of what the networks are after came to a head in that symbolic nine minutes. But I think the net winner by far was Bush. At that time he was still being widely thought of as a wimp. And here he had shot it out with "Dirty Dan" at "Dry Gulch Crick" [smiling]—and he'd come out a man, you know, and he'd certainly landed a punch on Rather or wounded him with the remark. I thought in the circumstances, considering the low blow, the fact that Rather kept his composure as well as he did was amazing.

Bush was criticized for taking "attack politics" too far during the '88 election. For instance, he accused Dukakis of wanting "kiddie pornography film legalized, movie rat-

ings systems canned." What do you think it says about Bush's character that he was willing to use those tactics in order to get into office?

I think clearly, one piece of him is extremely opportunistic . . . that ends are more important than means. And that says something about a person. I think the only thing you can say is, what does it say about a person's values that he will campaign in that manner? I think it makes it clear that part of his character—it's not the whole part, but part of his character—is a willingness to be very opportunistic.

Bush may rationalize to himself, "Look, I'm an honorable man, and I understand this country very well. And I know what it needs, and it needs me"—most political leaders think the country needs them [smiling]—"and it's trivial and inconsequential that I had to land some low blows against an inadequate Democratic candidate in order to get here, where my experience and good judgment, my hand on the helm will see this country safely through." I can imagine him rationalizing, if he were asked, that way.

When you are judging presidential candidates, how much do you personally feel you need to know about their private lives to evaluate them?

I'm fascinated. I'm fascinated to know, personally [smiling] . . . like anybody else, I'm dying to know all the gossip about anybody. I don't think that those parts of a man's life that he wishes to keep private are relevant. And if he's normal, he wants to keep his sexual life, for example, private. If he doesn't want to keep it private, that says something about him. And it's relevant to the campaign if it's relevant to the campaign. I think that's really what it comes down to. Clearly, Gary Hart's became relevant to the campaign. Should it not have become? There was almost an Aristotelian sense of fate hanging over that revelation.

Many candidates blame television news for flooding campaigns with stories about candidates' private lives and charge that it injures the political process. What do you think?

Well, I think that's a very narrow and self-serving view of it. Yes, broadcast journalism has failed to a certain extent; it hasn't lived up to the rather idealistic hopes that some had for it. To suggest that the politicians don't have some complicity in this is absurd.

What it is, is a kind of symbiosis between the two. The politicians naturally discovered and exploited the new opportunities in the wedding of nationwide television with the mass consumer opinion survey and sales techniques perfected by Madison Avenue, at the same time as television found it increasingly convenient to shorten the attention span—to keep things very brisk and bright and active and visual and violent—for it's own audience-getting purposes.

And it was a kind of wedding in hell, in a way, for the consumer, in this case the American voter. So there is a complicity between the two which makes it impossible for one to blame it on the other—although there will be seminar after seminar in which protagonists on both sides attempt to blame it on the other.

If you go back and read the history of the first televised debate, the Kennedy-Nixon one—both Kennedy and Nixon's negotiators got into very, very great detail. And Salinger, in his book *With Kennedy*, is very open about that. They wanted the press as interlocutors because they thought that if Kennedy himself came on too strong to Nixon, he would be perceived as the evil prosecutor, as the unsympathetic prosecutor. And that was the first time that format was used. And so he put the dirty stuff in the hands of the press. They're the ones who had to ask all the nasty questions and it's been that way ever since.

If the campaign perceives that it's going to get shafted by the reporter—now the reporter may be just doing a legitimate job—the campaign will be driven to more and more inventive and intoxicating photo opportunities. I'll give you an example. George Bush goes to the flag factory. The networks say, "Look at this! He's actually going to a flag factory!" And "Isn't this blatant?" And "Isn't this obvious?" Whether or not they said that, there is the president with flags all around *on the networks* for a minute, two minutes.

And nothing can undo the indelible psychic impression created in the minds of the audience, almost subliminally, by the picture of George Bush with a lot of flags. It was the most brilliant and cynical bit of manipulation of the media. And the longer they took to complain about how they were being manipulated, and how blatant it was, the more George Bush was shown with pictures of flags.

Do you think the increased influence of "new" news forms, such as talk shows, that we saw in the '92 campaign is a good thing for the political process?

Sure. Anything that widens interest in politics and especially whets the curiosity of people who don't pay that much attention to the traditional news outlets, I think is healthy for democracy. I don't see why politics in any sense should be the preserve of the "sacred, initiated priesthood" who are political reporters on television or in the newspapers. In fact, for a lot of people, that's a big turnoff because they see them as part of the system.

And I think any theory of democracy would applaud using the latest communications technology of the age to widen the access to politics, either in the CNN or C-SPAN form of letting people have a window on things as they're actually happening, and not through the filter of journalistic compression and selection, or through the talk-show format that Clinton used so well and that Ross Perot used so effectively. It has the weakness of allowing politicians to escape tough and informed questions and sometimes rather naive and overpolite questions of ordinary voters, but that's healthy too. The press can get very arrogant and self-important about its well-informed questions as you frequently see in presidential news conferences.

Is there some kind of snobbery about pop culture that runs through criticisms of talk shows?

Oh, sure there is, and anybody who is part of the "guild" and who's served the time and paid the initiation dues to the "ancient and honorable guild" of people qualified to talk about politics obviously hates it that other people who aren't initiated can do it. But that's the essence of democracy actually. I think everybody—no matter how simple a person in his education and daily life—every human being acquires some ability to judge the character of other human beings.

Television is a wonderful kind of artificial window on our leaders and it does allow people to judge. And they do. If you believe in democracy, you believe that the judgments of a lot of very ordinary and unsophisticated people are valuable. And I think television makes them spectators and puts them in a position to judge, whether the person is tossing off one-liners to the press or whether he is answering pleasant, but fairly soft questions of voters in a talk show. The positive thing about the talk show is it brings people to the spectator's window and puts them in a position to judge and form some opinion.

Have you ever felt compelled to publicly voice your views about a presidential candidate in your broadcasts?

No. No. Because, covering presidential candidates I've gone back and forth. I've just done my best to explain that candidate as well as I could. And then if I jumped over to the other candidate, I did my best to explain him, and to get inside the skin of that person.

I was asked a question by a businessman the other day in circumstances that annoyed me . . . "Why *can't* a journalist be objective?" And I said, "It is just as easy for a journalist to be objective as it is for a businessman to be honest" [smiling] . . . which he didn't like. It's just as easy and just as difficult. But, you know, 99 percent of it is intention. If we have as one of the essential criteria for *MacNeil/Lehrer* to be objective, it also means we fail now and then, but, if you're making the effort, most of the time you will be.

I don't think it is outside human nature to be objective. The function of a modern journalist in this age is to present the alternatives to the voter, and try and make them vibrant and interesting and relevant. And I think that it's quite possible to do that and be fair. One of my proudest possessions is a picture I have, signed by Barry Goldwater, who called me a "fair and objective man" after I'd covered him for a whole year. And, you know, there was a general assumption in the country that the so-called Eastern Liberal Press—he actually gave us little gold pins that said, "Eastern Liberal Press"—could not be fair to that man.

It's a different question—*should* journalists be objective? One can argue that there are times when it is more important that they not be. For instance, I felt during the Vietnam War that a lot of journalists, particularly television journalists, were carrying their "above the fray" posture too far, because the . . . survival, not the survival, but certainly the good health of this country was seriously at risk.

The Vietnam War did more damage to this country than anything has since the Civil War. Television became a kind of cheerleader for the status quo, because television could *show* the war, because that was the animal television was. And it went that way very far before it swung back the other way. There weren't any *MacNeil / Lehrer* news hours at the time or anything like it. There was hardly ever any analysis or discussion on television, and not enough examination given to "Is this a war the United States should be in?"

There are moments of national peril, of enormous peril or concern, when anybody's going to feel, "Hey wait a minute, it's time to declare what I feel"—my citizenship or my love of country or my sense of what is shameful. And that was my feeling at the time. I was strongly opposed to the war from the beginning. I was working for NBC and a certain amount of that leaked out as it did in all our work. I know it did, in the skeptical tone that I took in a number of those essays.

What do you say to the view that "all this talk about the media and politics" is unnecessary, that politics has always been rough and tumble, journalists have always extracted short quotes?

You can make that argument and I can understand that argument, but it leaves out one facet which wasn't present in the old days of dirty campaigning in the nineteenth century and dirty campaigning earlier in this century through the medium of the printed press. And that is, television can reach far more people and it reaches most effectively the people who aren't interested in politics, who are the least educated and have the smallest party identification or loyalty, who are a shifting sand of loyalty from election to election, who are the swing vote.

There is a much greater potential of impact through television. Why does Detroit put so much money into selling cars on television, if it's not on a different order of effectiveness in their minds than print? So, I think that destroys that argument. If the person who said that is not alarmed by the direction the political discourse has taken in this democracy (and what you can at least argue are the consequences of the election techniques now), then I would be very surprised. And think that that person was extremely cynical or indifferent, if he would think that there is no difference in the quality of politics today—from 1964, 1960, 1956, 1948, 1944, 1930. . . . Really? I would find that amazing. I would find that disturbingly cynical.

What about the view that low voter participation is a sign of a contented populace, that it doesn't have to do with voter reactions to the media?

Well, I have no way of measuring how much it's a reaction to the style of campaigns. I have some feelings about it, but there's no way to be precise about it. I find that a bizarre reading. In other words, the country is more and more contented? The logic of that would be, each presidential election since 1960, the voters of this country have been more and more contented. . . . I mean, that's crazy.

You have a country which parades itself to the world [as]—and is—the leading democracy. And something like 25 percent of its population is excluded from active participation in anything, and then you say that that population is contented? I think alienated might be a better explanation. Now, whether they're alienated because of the style of campaigning, or because they feel that the electoral system no longer gives them any stake, or that they feel it's irrelevant to them—I would think that huge numbers of people feel that the system is irrelevant to them. I find that bizarre . . . perverse.

Why do you think character issues are so important in presidential campaigns?

Well, character issues are almost built into the presidential system and television has just made that easier and

easier, or worse and worse, whatever you like. Television
has further personified American government in the president, in the body and person and family and comings and
goings of the president—the personality of the president.
It's almost made it inevitable. And that's built into the
system, that the president is dramatized and is the figure-
head.

And people long for that anyway in a country where you
don't have a king or you don't have some kind of mythic
figure to identify with—the president gets that kind of
identification, quite understandably. It's bad at times and
it's good at times. It can be extremely helpful. Take something like the *Challenger* tragedy. I mean, it is wonderful,
on a night like that, when a man like Reagan—whatever
else you think about him—can in five or six minutes read
a speech of such enormous eloquence and empathy, that
the country feels drawn together and shares a moment in
which its anger and its fear and its sense of disappointment can somehow be experienced cathartically. Now if
you didn't have a president who had that kind of personi-
fication of the whole country, that wouldn't be as easy.

Carter had the potential and did in some ways reintro-
duce a kind of Jeffersonian idea of the president as the
kind of nonimperial citizen who comes in, and he's no
better than anybody else for a while, and then leaves and
goes back to his farm. He happened to do that at a time
when some hunger for a grand, if not imperial, president
was still there in the national spirit.

*What do you think of the contention that Reagan's suc-
cess with the media in "emphasizing the positive" gave the
public a false impression that things were getting better in
America?*

That is much too simple. I mean the reality of this country
is so incredibly complex that . . . leadership is in part being
able to grasp the sort of psychic tone of your country at a

particular time and respond to it and carry it in some direction. Or merely just respond to it. Reagan may have merely just responded to it. These are the kinds of things I don't talk about easily. But I think the interesting ingredient that's relevant is, How much did Reagan fool the American people and how much did he simply play into their wishes? Were they misled by the nature of his campaigning or were they led into ways they wanted to go? Was Reagan a sort of modern pied piper?

It's my instinct about it that he very successfully delayed the apprehension of reality by this country for about a decade. He made people feel that things were better than they were, that the external dangers were greater than they were. I think the jury's out on a lot of that and my own feeling about it is that the evil that that did on delaying making this country really competitive with the rest of the world and so on—may have to be balanced in history by the success that Reagan appears to have had, maybe accidentally, with the Soviet Union . . . which is a very, very complicated business.

All the news media have a sense of a president's popularity and it creates a climate; it creates weather. If a president's popularity goes up, there's a kind of high pressure area around him, the sun shines, skies are blue. And the media can't help reflecting that. They are aware of a president's popularity, so there is a natural tendency to jump on him less hard when a president is popular and jump on him harder when he isn't popular. It just happens. Because, "Why isn't he popular? Because he's screwing up. Why's he screwing up?" On, on, on, on. All this stuff. Sometimes there's a reverse tendency, because a man is so popular to test him even harder, you know, it's part of journalistic machismo.

There is another factor at work though, and this is a longer term factor. Ever since the press, and through it the country, was lied to over, first, Vietnam and then Watergate, there's been a mood in the press of aggressive hostility. It used to be assumed thirty years ago that by and large, if the president said something the chances were, he was telling the truth. It's like the Anglo-Roman system of justice: you're innocent until you're proved guilty. I think part of the disillusionment of the press, and part of its own self-protection—"Boy, we're never going to be lied to again. We're never going to have the wool pulled over our eyes again!"—was a demeanor that implied "You're lying until it's demonstrated you're telling the truth." Now I think that eased off during the Reagan years. Also the press liked Reagan a lot. Whether a man's popular or not, the press has a collective sense of "they like this guy."

But there was also tension?

Yeah, because they couldn't get to him; he wouldn't say anything. They had those carefully staged little ballets on the lawn as he went to the helicopter . . . the weekly little piece of theater between Donaldson and Reagan, which worked wonderfully to Reagan's advantage. Donaldson personified the "nasty, hostile, aggressive press." "Goodness! Couldn't this decent nice old man go off for a quiet weekend without being snapped and yapped by these people?" And of course it was all staged! If the president hadn't wanted to be snapped at, he could have gone over and chatted with them a little bit. If he hadn't wanted to be shouted at, he could have turned the helicopter rotors off. But he didn't. It was all a little ballet staged to give the impression that he wanted to communicate, but here were these people beating up on him all the time.

They could have in that case simply ignored that situation—watched the president and not shouted and not played into that little scenario. That White House managed a brilliant piece of image manipulation, which broke down only a few times. Very difficult for the press to break through that. But then the fact that Mr. Reagan was president was the consequence of the 1980 election. How does a man like Ronald Reagan become president of the United States? Because he can use the system of the present machinery of politics very well. Without television would Ronald Reagan have been elected president of the United States? I doubt it very much.

The office has become an office of public relations management and news management in the television age, going back to Kennedy. And so the way of getting to the office has become more of an attempt to manage the news and control the environment you want your potential voter to perceive. And increasingly, it's apparent that campaigning skill is the paramount ingredient in getting elected, and the qualifications for the office are secondary to that—to being able to create your sense of reality. And that is what a candidate does; he creates his sense of reality.

How would you compare Clinton to Reagan regarding their campaigning skill and their qualifications for the office?

Well, you have a high degree of correlation in campaigning skills and the communicating skills they bring to the office. They're both brilliant at it and wonderful both in television and in person. Since Kennedy, they are the very peak in the television age of that kind of ability. It's much harder to judge the skills they bring to the office.

Reagan was consistently underestimated by the normal criteria. Reporters and political scientists and colleagues and everybody measuring him by the usual criteria wondered whether he was qualified at all. His time in the presidency convinced a lot of people, on a basic visceral level, he was highly qualified to run this country. George Shultz has just published a memoir which makes that point repeatedly about Reagan, that his innate, deep sense of the country and what he thought was right for it, made him, although not a hands-on or detailed president, very, very effective.

I don't think that a mere empty vessel of an actor, however skilled, could have entranced the American public to the degree that he did for eight years. I mean, we are not that much susceptible to mass hypnosis. I think Reagan was giving us a message many people wanted to hear, and it was a very hopeful, positive message. But Ronald Reagan could say something like "It's morning in America," and people thought there was some substance in it. Because they wanted to. A lot of leadership is the ability to absorb the projections of the people who want to be led, the transference and projections of their own hopes and fears and anxieties and understanding of the country. And Reagan was very good at that and I think Clinton has an enormous amount of that same ability.

NOTES

1. MacNeil, Robert, *The Right Place at the Right Time* (Boston: Little, Brown, and Company, 1982), p. 295.

2. *Ibid.*, p. 290.

3. *Ibid.*, p. 286.

4. *Ibid.*, p 266.

5. *Ibid.*, p. 266–67.

Gittings/Skipworth, Inc.

2

LINDA ELLERBEE

Linda Ellerbee is a syndicated columnist and President of Lucky Duck Productions.

Quick-witted and unquestionably frank, Linda Ellerbee is one of broadcast journalism's most candid critics. The author of the best-selling memoir *And So It Goes*, a funny, irreverent look at broadcast journalism, Ellerbee is well known for her revelations about the inside workings of TV news.

Ellerbee's canny, unrestrained criticism of the news business and her sometimes very personal testimonies on issues such as abortion and motherhood have earned her a reputation as a journalist who brings an extra measure of forthrightness to her work. Many viewers find her just a little bit more "real" than other TV journalists, someone who has been unwilling to neutralize herself in favor of a more polished image. Ellerbee's career has been rife with gestures that counter news anchors' tendencies toward self-aggrandizement: the yellow duck she kept perched on the news desk of NBC's late night news program *Overnight*; her habit of arriving at work in T-shirts, Reeboks, and jeans; and her coasting into the austere, marble-floored lobby of NBC News on a pair of roller skates the day after one of her newsmagazines was axed.

Nor has she kept her own less-than-lofty beginnings in the news business a secret. A child of the sixties, Ellerbee dropped out of Vanderbilt University in 1964 and spent several years living in a commune and traveling about the Southwest. Her ambitions to be a journalist first surfaced when she was fired from her job at a radio station in Alaska. "It was as simple as could be: I needed the money," she recalls in her autobiography. "I found myself in Juneau, Alaska, without a job, without a husband, without an education—but *with* a three-year-old daughter and a two-year-old son to raise. Then I became a journalist."[1]

For a while Ellerbee worked as a speech writer and wrote dozens of letters to newspapers and radio stations in the Southwest, looking for work. She wanted to go back to Texas, her home state. The Dallas Bureau of the Associated Press wrote back and told her that though she didn't have a degree or any experience, if she passed their qualification tests, she might be able to get a job. The only hitch was she had to take the tests in Dallas. So Ellerbee drove with her kids to Dallas, got a copy of the reading list for the basic journalism course at the local university, and spent two days and nights in a motel room cramming for the exams.

Ellerbee passed the exams and worked the better part of a year for the Associated Press in Dallas, and then for a local TV station in Houston. In 1973, Eric Ober, the news director of the CBS affiliate in New York City, saw some tapes of Ellerbee's reports on a series of Texas murders and invited her to New York to work for him at WCBS-TV. She spent the next two years trouping about New York City with a television crew, covering local hard news—riots, fires, and murders—for the eleven-o'clock broadcasts. Then in 1975, she signed on with NBC.

The next eleven years, often referred to as "The Perils of Linda," were a dizzying mix of success and failure.

Though Ellerbee garnered a lot of attention, three news-magazines which she co-anchored were cancelled out from under her—*Weekend, Overnight,* and *Summer Sunday.* In 1986, despite her memoir's flight on the bestseller charts, NBC asked her to take a 40 percent cut in pay. In a highly publicized move, Ellerbee opted for an offer from ABC to anchor the prime time news program *Our World* with Ray Gandolf. Running up against the ratings blockbuster *The Cosby Show, Our World* fared poorly and ran less than a year. Ellerbee left ABC and started her own production company, whimsically named Lucky Duck Productions.

Since starting the production company Ellerbee has endured many struggles. At first Lucky Duck was hard up for projects, and in order to keep it going Ellerbee accepted an offer from Maxwell House in 1988 to do a coffee commercial, a gesture for which she drew much criticism. In 1991 Ellerbee published her second book, the semi-auto-biographical *Move On,* and Lucky Duck Productions slowly but surely found success. Among its productions are the award-winning program on AIDS for children, *A Conversation with Magic,* which featured Magic Johnson, and *Nick News,* a Nickelodeon newsmagazine for kids, which Ellerbee produces, writes, and hosts.

Throughout Ellerbee has maintained her candor about the business she works in and her own personal struggles, including her recoveries from alcoholism and breast cancer. As quick as she is to make a joke, she is equally quick to talk directly about issues with a refreshing lack of restraint. Ellerbee will often say what others are willing only to imply.

Television journalists are often accused of having so much influence on presidential campaigns, that they play too big a role. What should their role be?

I tell you, I wish I had an answer to that, I really do. It has become so complicated and television is not entirely to blame here. The politicians are equally to blame. It has been a kind of love affair that gives unsafe sex a good name, really [laughing]. . . . I mean, politicians and journalists have conspired, particularly in television, to completely twist out of shape the American electoral process, and to render useless certain methods of choosing a president. It's made it so that we cannot see anything accurately because of the image getting in the way—it's mutual use, and the loser is the American public.

Politicians know how. They've read our book—they know how to play to us. And unfortunately we buy into it. We bring out the worst in each other, television and politics; we truly do. It'd be almost impossible to have a good presidential debate on television now. First of all, they're no longer debates. You have these negotiators like countries doing treaties, who sit around and decide who will ask the questions, and how high the podium will be, and where the cameras will be—I'm serious—and what color ties they will wear.

Well, what that adds up to is advertising—we are talking about image. And that is the whole problem of television and politics—that politicians, historically, have understood that it didn't matter how good they were, if they weren't perceived as good. And it didn't matter very often how bad they were as long as they were perceived as good. Image. Image. Well, along comes television, the biggest image machine in history! No wonder. When was the last time you actually saw a candid moment of a politician on television? And as I say, it's not all their fault and it's not all our fault.

You need to put a critical distance between yourself and that which you see on television. Be it the reporter or the politician. To watch television is to be constantly on one's guard, if you would be a good citizen. Be skeptical. Now that's not cynical. Skeptical. You should give politicians the benefit of the doubt. You should doubt, but you shouldn't judge them ahead of time. But what you should always try and do is measure what they are saying against what they're doing.

Talk shows are touted as being more direct and less prone to image management. Do you think that's true?

Well, it's very clear that one of the reasons that the candidates went around ABC, CBS . . . went around Sam Donaldson, and straight to the talk shows is because Larry King doesn't ask as hard a question. He's a nice guy, but he ain't the questioner Sam Donaldson is. So it suited their interests in every way to do that.

So are talk shows the media manager's version of heaven?

Absolutely! Maury Povich is not Mike Wallace and that was not lost on a single candidate . . . to get away from the regular media, and it was interesting because it was not altogether bad. It really wasn't. As much as in any time in memory the people set the agenda in 1992. Not the reporters and not even the politicians. From the very beginning of the campaign it seemed that people were saying to politicians, "We don't want your stinking photo ops, we don't want your negative ads, we don't want your spin doctors. Answer our questions. Give us answers or good-bye."

And I think they went on saying that until the politicians, left with little recourse, actually started to have to begin to do this. No, they never did answer some of our most basic questions. I mean, did Bill Clinton ever really explain how he could tax only the rich and provide more programs and decrease the deficit? No, he didn't. Did George Bush ever really explain what his program to fix the economy was, or why he didn't have one for four years? No, he didn't. And Ross Perot—who understood so very well that getting people to laugh was easier than getting them to think—did he ever really explain what he'd do if we gave him the job? No, he didn't. None of them answered those questions.

Plus there were still too many polls. And from the press, still too much horse-race handicapping. Yet throughout the campaign the people refused again and again to let the politicians or the journalists sink to their natural level [laughing] if you will, and they even met with some success. There was more talk of issues this year and all because there was more involvement by the people.

Do you think there was some genuine effort at reform by journalists after the 1988 campaign?

I think we all looked around after '88 and said, "Achh, we have got to do this better. Something must be done." And those TV and radio talk and call-in shows may not have been the traditional road, but, talk they did and call in people did with questions that were often tougher than those asked by the "Larry Kings" and the "Maury Povichs."

So, while I don't think they were the greatest interviewers, I think a lot of the people on their shows were. I think it was on some call-in show, it was the only time I heard anyone ask Ross Perot the most obvious question of all, which is, "Do you think people would listen to you for more than two minutes if you didn't have two billion dollars?"

Do you think that over time, if candidates are in front of cameras day after day after day, the viewers do get a feeling for the candidate?

Well, I could argue either side of that because both are true. I remember in '80 doing a story on Ronald Reagan shooting a campaign commercial. And he was shooting it in a grocery store in Lima, Ohio. Now, granted, he didn't know we were a network crew that was in there; he thought we were another production crew hired to make his commercial. Jim Baker knew we were a network crew and he had told the Reagans, but because I don't dress like most people on television [laughing], they forgot who we were.

And in the course of that commercial Ronald Reagan blew his lines eight times and the director yelled at him. So did his wife. And that piece aired on the news, and *The Washington Post* wrote a story about it. The piece just got all kinds of noise made about it because some people said, "You made the candidate look like a fool!"

Other people said, and I was one of the people who felt this way, "No, it really gave just a more natural glimpse of the man." And in fact, I thought, and some other people thought, that it gave a picture of a man being jerked around by television producers. But for a moment you at least got through the glass wall to see a little bit of Ronald Reagan, the human being, which I felt was valuable.

What do you think of Ross Perot?

I think he's a dangerous man. I think people who come in and tell you what's wrong and don't tell you how they're going to fix it have the absolute easiest road and that's the road he took. I don't think Ross Perot actually believes in a free press—I think Ronald Reagan believed more in a free press than Ross Perot [laughing].

I think he's a very dangerous, dangerous man. The Ross Perots of the world—that's how you get Hitlers. You know, you get people who come in with seemingly easy answers. And, you know what? Not even the questions are easy these days. He says, "I'll just make the government smaller, and that'll fix everything! We'll just run it like we run a company." Well, a company and a government are not the same thing. It's very different running a company to suit yourself, and running a country to suit 200 million people! I also found his tactics of spying on employees more than questionable: I found that outright offensive. That kind of thing. Of course, as a Texan, this is not my first experience with short, bombastic white men.

Many charge that the national press has a liberal bias. Do you think that's true?

I would deny that charge vehemently. The press is not liberal. The national press is centrist if it's anything, other than editorial writers and columnists, which we'll have to leave aside for the moment. The national press has for some years sought the centrist position in any given issue and gone with it. And part of this comes, in television, from the pressure that is on you constantly, to remember who your audience is, "Middle America" they say to you, as if that means, "middle-brained" or "middle thought" [laughing].

The press sought the center in everything. Not just in their writing style, but in their politics as well. They began to play to the middle of thought, not the lowest, not the highest, not the most left, not the most right. The very middle. And it's fine when you're doing it to be fair. But when it becomes self-censorship, it's no damn good.

I'm much more acutely aware of this now that I write a newspaper column, because I do criticize. And I have found myself writing a column and saying, "Is this just too far off base; I'm going against what everybody else in America says. . . ." Then I stop and think, "Well, what do I care? I'm being paid for my opinion here. I'm not running a popularity contest anymore." But *networks* are constantly running a popularity contest. And by definition that means reporters are.

What about bias during presidential campaigns?

You run into different problems in presidential campaigns too. I mean, when you have one person covering a candidate from start to finish, after a while they either feel aligned with them or . . . it's almost the Stockholm syndrome, you know, the way people begin to feel aligned with their kidnappers? When you're locked on a bus or an airplane with somebody [laughing] for several months, you start to almost feel aligned with them, particularly in the early days of the campaign, when your fortunes rise or fall by the fortunes of that candidate.

After a while it's possible that you end up feeling aligned with them or that you end up *hating* that person. It's not quite so much that you take to their views, but their views certainly become so familiar to you that, in the sense that you may not like everybody in your family, but after a while, you know them so well that some of their views get reflected in yours.

But Ronald Reagan, by everybody's definition, was the Teflon president, and it wasn't that the media tried to touch him and failed. The media didn't try that hard. So where's your "elitist liberal media"? Nobody was as fast to come down on Mike Dukakis as the media were. On almost every issue. I mean, they chewed him up. Nobody was as hard on Jimmy Carter as the media were, and certainly nobody was as hard on Geraldine Ferraro. If you're a liberal, the idea of a woman candidate is wonderful. And yet, my lord, the press was all over that woman, *and her husband*, in ways that they have not been all over male candidates.

Jimmy Carter's presidency was just completely chewed up by the media. Look, I'll give you the biggest example going, and I know other people in the business who actually believe that Jimmy Carter could have survived the hostage situation if it weren't for a little thing called *Nightline*. The fact that every single night there was ABC going on the air for half an hour, talking about this one story, that by implication Jimmy Carter had messed up, was probably as big a factor as anything else in that campaign.

Now I do not think that this was malicious on the part of ABC. I don't think that anybody said, "Here's a way to get Jimmy Carter." I think it was legitimate on ABC's part to do that. But I think this is a perfect example of refuting the charge of the liberal media. With Dukakis, I can tell you firsthand that the general feeling among reporters was—there was no love for Michael Dukakis; there was this feeling that this man wasn't up to the task. Which doesn't necessarily translate to a love for George Bush, but once again goes against the argument that we're a liberal media.

And was that justified in your mind?

Yes, I think it was. I may not be a George Bush fan, but I was damn glad Michael Dukakis was not trying to handle the whole Gulf situation. And look, everybody talks about the "liberal media"—I voted for Ronald Reagan in 1980. And I'm one of those people that if anybody gets accused of being liberal, it's me. I voted for Ronald Reagan!

I voted for Ronald Reagan because in covering the Carter campaign that year, as the Carter people towards the end began to perceive themselves to be losing, they began to behave like rats in heat. Stupid things like, if you wrote a story they didn't like, they'd leave your luggage in the town you were leaving that day to go to the next one. Or they'd come and they'd, you know, they'd start yelling at you about something you'd written.

I'm not going to get into the names at this point—everybody's got to go on to another job—but toward the public's lead.

Television perceived that Ronald Reagan's view was the view of 95 percent of the people in America. And I do not think that was true. But that was the perception. When we were doing *Overnight* at NBC News, which went on at 1:30 in the morning, one of the things we did, was to go to all the people that covered Ronald Reagan, or that covered

Washington in all aspects, and we said to them, "If you feel your pieces are being too chopped up"—for whatever reasons, not just politically—"do the piece as you felt it should have been done and we will play it uncut on *Overnight*." And we got an awful lot of good stuff out of reporters.

And in the course of that, and I want to emphasize that not all of this was politically motivated—they felt sometimes, you know, "They just cut my piece for time. . . ." But in the course of that, we also got pieces that were far more critical of Ronald Reagan than nightly news was ever running.

How much of the strong leader we saw in the television images of Ronald Reagan do you think was really there?

With Reagan you always wondered who was pulling the strings. You had this "nice Mr. Reagan" with a bedside manner for a dying nation. But then you wondered, Who's running the country? He appeared to be a strong leader, yes, and he was strong in the sense of not backing down— but I did not think that he was the one calling the shots all the time.

Did you feel that way about Bush?

Not to that extent. Look, any president is going to have advisers and rely on them; otherwise why have them? But I didn't get the puppet feeling that I did with Reagan. And I think that did contribute to that Teflon presidency. "Why blame that nice man? He's not even making these decisions." Well somebody should blame him for that! I mean, I think the American people have a perfect right to ask and to get an answer to the question, "Who's in charge here?"

One of the reasons they held so few press conferences is the man could not be relied on to know the facts. So, who was making those decisions? I think Bush was more his own man. You know, that's why he held more news conferences, not a lot, but more. He was able to answer questions—"I've just made this decision; now you ask me questions about it." You couldn't do that with Ronald Reagan. He couldn't answer questions about decisions a lot of the time, because he didn't understand them.

I don't think he was stupid, but he was lazy. He was lazy and, look, he was beginning to get senile and I think the press protected him a lot on that, and certainly his handlers protected him every way they could. Why? Because you get into the human area. Everybody has parents, your parents get old, it's no sin to start really forgetting things, to start losing some of your faculties. To come down on a man because of that makes you pretty evil.

But the problem is, this man was president of the United States. And the fact is, we do protect those in power. Look at Betty Ford's drinking. There's the perfect example. Do you think the press corps didn't know that Betty Ford was a drunk? Of course they did; of course *we* did. Betty Ford and I have talked about this.

She's a recovering alcoholic, and she can laugh about it now and say that the fact that her drinking was protected kept her drinking that much longer, kept her from getting sober that much sooner. So it sure did her no service. But the feeling was, she wasn't the president; she was the president's wife; you know, she had a problem, it was a personal problem, the nation didn't have a problem. But with Reagan, the nation had a problem.

But it's never simple. I can recall at no time anyone in high management of NBC saying, "Don't be hard on Ronald Reagan." It was really more the perception that Ronald Reagan spoke for all of America, and that if you wanted to be the most popular newscast in America, you obviously should reflect what all America thinks.

Did the increased pressure to make money in the late seventies and early eighties, to get better ratings, affect your work?

Oh well that's certainly true. There's always been some pressure, but never as much as now. You had ABC and CBS both change hands during that time, and NBC. All three of them changed hands and with the new hands came "new hands on" policy if you will. Let's take *Our World*. There's a very good example. *Our World* went on the air in 1986. It replaced a show called *Ripley's Believe It or Not*.

Ripley's Believe It or Not cost a million dollars a week to produce and it got an eight rating, something like that. They said, "Here's our idea. *Our World* will cost four hundred thousand dollars a week to produce; if you get at least an eight rating, we will make that much more money, because it won't cost as much to produce." So we went on the air. We got even better than an eight rating. They came back a year later and said, "It's not enough."

It all goes back to the caveat that news had to make money. It probably didn't start there, but it's when it became open. Let me give an example that doesn't have to do with news, but it indirectly has to do with this. Recently we did a pilot for a network, and we showed it to the network and they said to me, "Can't you make it more exploitive?" And I said, "Excuse me? I thought that was a word that if you used at all, you used in secret and to one another. The fact that you feel perfectly open in saying this to me shows me such a change, and I am so frightened by this."

And they said, "Ah! Well, we don't know what you mean" [laughing]. So, what has happened, was that over the years that word had become somehow acceptable. Over the years in *news* it has now become acceptable that news must make money; it's no longer even an argument. In the beginning of the seventies, it was still an argument, whether news ought to have to make money. No more. Now it's just how much.

But I don't blame television. Remember, during this whole thing, it's very important to make the distinction of not blaming television. It's not television. It is the combination of television and politics. It's a dirty little marriage.

I remember once when I was doing a story on military preparedness for *NBC Nightly News* years ago. And I was interviewing some navy admiral. And they were talking about why you couldn't allow women on ships—the problems that were caused. And I finally stopped the man and I said, "You're not looking at this right. These problems are not caused by women on ships. These problems are caused by the combination of men and women on ships." So that's why when you're talking about television and politics, you always got to go back to "These problems aren't caused by television, they're caused by the combination of television and politics."

NOTE

1. Ellerbee, Linda, *And So It Goes* (New York: G. P. Putnam's Sons, 1986), p. 10.

3

LARRY KING

Larry King is the host of CNN's *Larry King Live.*

When Ross Perot told Larry King he'd consider running for president if voters got him on the ballot in fifty states, *Larry King Live* became a political hot spot. That night CNN phone lines jammed with viewers wanting to contact Perot—the start of Perot's 1992 presidential bid. In the months that followed candidates Bush, Clinton, Gore, Perot, and Quayle all appeared on *Larry King Live*, interviews that were so high-profile that King was often dubbed the "MC of the '92 Election" and the "man who gave the country Ross Perot."

Along with the hype came an onslaught of criticism. As talk shows wielded more clout, criticism of them increased, and *Larry King Live* drew considerable fire. The charges were formidable—that King's probing, but "soft" interviewing style was inappropriate for interrogating political candidates; that his show was the perfect place for candidates to escape the scrutiny of more traditional journalists; that King failed to follow up on specific claims by candidates; and that allegations and attacks waged on his show got wide play without a shred of evidence.

Critics also made the point that while talk shows like King's are touted as offering a direct pipeline to candidates, they aren't really that democratic, that only the most vocal and opinionated participate. And as if the charges of pandering to candidates and letting gossip and innuendo air unchallenged weren't enough, another charge was that *Larry King Live* was the ideal setting for a politician to exploit public frustration with oversimplistic rhetoric—a breeding ground for demagoguery. In the minds of some, just such a demagogue did just that: Ross Perot.

So Larry King, the man "who gave us Ross Perot," is no stranger to controversy. And while criticism of his interviewing style is biting, there is also much to be said in defense of it. King is quick to counter that he is an interviewer, not a journalist. What he delivers is the candidate in front the camera, unedited, answering questions. And in the course of an hour or two, a lot can be revealed about a candidate. There are plenty of "Ted Koppels" and "Mike Wallaces" to grill candidates on specifics. Why shouldn't the public get another angle on the candidates?

As to the criticism that King is a fawning interviewer— his guests have revealed themselves in ways that attest to the advantages of his style. It was during the course of one of King's chatty, loose-knit interviews that Bush admitted to "Iraqgate," that he had knowledge of American loan guarantees being used by Iraq to buy military technology. Dan Quayle, a staunchly prolife candidate, told King that he'd support his daughter if she decided to have an abortion, revealing a decidedly human side.

Americans are acutely aware that candidates are more than ideas, that they're human beings, and that as a nation we have a vested interest in the character of our president. Our disappointment with Nixon had nothing to do with his command of the issues; Reagan's foreign policy successes were not divorced from his character. And what venue might give us a glimpse of those "intangible" elements of personality and character? Among others, King's meandering, intuitive interviewing style.

And however opinionated or vocal the people are who call in to talk shows, they are citizens and they are *talking* to the candidates. Some questions are soft, but some are tough. Nor is it unthinkable that distaste for talk shows like King's is fueled in part by rivalries between print and electronic media, and between more traditional journalists and the "New News" forms that proliferated in 1992. "You know why I can stiff you on the press conferences?" President Clinton quipped at a correspondents' dinner, "because Larry King liberated me from you by giving me to the American people directly."[1] King did not "pay his dues" academically or on the campaign trail. The fact that he commanded so much clout in a presidential campaign made some people's heads spin. But it is also part of King's populist appeal to viewers—he is "like us," not "them."

What King has experience in is "doing talk," and King has been doing talk for a long time. In 1956, King was twenty-three when he started as a D.J. for a Miami Beach radio station. Just before he went on the air the manager suggested he change his last name to "King"—"Ziegler" was too German, too Jewish. King moved on to host a radio interview show, broadcast from a famous Miami restaurant, and then landed his own television interview show.

King's success crumbled in 1971 when he was arrested for larceny.[2] At the time he was also a chronic gambler and over a quarter-million dollars in debt. Because of the statute of limitations, the larceny case never went to trial,[3] but King was bounced off the air and wouldn't find steady work until 1975, when a Miami radio station hired him. His big break came when *The Larry King Show*, the first national talk show, went on the air in 1978. In 1985 Ted

Turner hired him to CNN and *Larry King Live* soon became CNN's top-rated show. King also writes a column for *USA Today* and has authored several autobiographical books. For nearly forty years he's been the consummate yakker—inquiring, prodding, and cajoling.

A conversation with Larry King is like a drive in the country with Mario Andretti. He's talking; you're talking. And yet every corner turned, every twist of phrase—no matter how easy the chatter, how rough the syntax—is arrestingly smooth. Amid the debates over talk shows and the celebrity hype, one element of King's interviews often slips by unattended. What does King have that singles him out from the legions of other talk show hosts? And why do so many viewers and guests find his interviews so engaging?

Perhaps Larry King is more than a fawning Mr. Schmooze; perhaps he often has what so many journalists strive for: a certain empathy or stopgap attentiveness that can be golden in many contexts, among friends or family or even in that strangely modern exchange, the electronic interview. Much can be said to criticize King's interviewing style and to defend it—ample rhetoric and points worth making for both sides. In the meantime King will do what he's always done, "doing talk."

Do you think talk-show formats are much more susceptible to manipulation by some sort of demagogue?

Absolutely, but what do you want to do about it?

Some say that you should change your style, that you should do interviews differently.

Well, some of the worst demagogues were before television. Television helped break down a demagogue. It brought down Joe McCarthy. You can only get so far with demagoguery when you're on every night, because the public's going to see through you. They'll spot a phony in the long run. You could be a fad, but in the long haul, you've got to have something going for you.

And we've had more demagogues before television than since. Television ruins the David Dukes. It presents them and ruins them. I think Hitler might have been a failure on television. Might not have been able to communicate well. Adversely Lincoln might have been a failure. I don't know. We'll never know that.

But that's also moot. There's nothing you can do about it. What are you going to do? Not put on the candidate? Do you know any sane person who would say, "No. I won't put you on"? No, of course not. Television is the way we communicate today. You don't communicate on television, you're a dead duck.

Some talk shows are terrible, some are good, some are terrific, some are tabloid, some are not. But you get such a wide choice—yeah, we have our "National Enquirer" talk shows, but also we have our "New York Times," we have our "Washington Post." Sure the effect of television is enormous, but it's moot to even talk about it, to stand in a corner and wring our hands, and say, "Television elects candidates." Of course it does. It's like saying, "Gee, I wish the sun would rise in the West this morning" [laughing]. There's no other medium that can touch it.

How would you compare your style of interviewing to Ted Koppel's?

I don't even think it's fair to compare. Ted is a news interviewer. He's there strictly for the journalism and the event. Ted said it best—we were having lunch one day and he said, "You're interested in the human factor, I'm interested in the event factor."

For example, Ted doesn't want his guests in the studio with him. If you're on *Nightline*, you're in another studio. I like'm right there. Ted said to me if we were covering a fire, he would ask the fireman, "What caused this fire?"

And I would ask the fireman, "Why'd he want to fight fires?" That's absolutely true. So we're apples and oranges.

Do you think American journalists are too aggressive towards presidential candidates?

No, I think, "to each his own." I enjoy Sam Donaldson. I love Mike Wallace. I think, "If you've got it, you've got it." Mike Wallace has it. I think I've got it. Sam Donaldson has it. Koppel has it. It could be a certain style. Wallace has a style that could be nerve-wracking. So what? It's just not *my style*. And the one thing you can't do is copy a style or give someone else your style. I couldn't do what Sam Donaldson does. He couldn't do what I do.

Some people say that you're a pushover—you don't ask challenging questions and that's why your guests enjoy being interviewed by you. Why do you think people like being interviewed by you?

I think what people like is my curiosity. It's not a curiosity based on a headline; it's not a curiosity based on who you slept with last night. I think people respect that I really am interested in them. It's not phony-baloney, light-hearted good humor with a band in the background; it's me. And they know, whether it's Bill Clinton or Bob Dole or Ross Perot or Richard Dreyfus, I *care* about what they say. It's not "soft."

I never learned anything, by the way, screaming at somebody. I never learned anything. You know when you create hostility—and that's very easy to do by the way—I never learn anything. I know how to argue. If you and I were having an emotional argument—now I know all the tricks, I know to undercut, I know how to gut hurt you. But I don't learn anything.

Curiosity makes me learn, and then through me, the audience learns. So it's just different than when a candidate's on *Meet the Press*. I know it's different; the audience knows it's different. I could give all these explanations, but at the end of it, there's something there that's happening and I don't know what it is. There's a human quality to it.

When you're doing an interview, what's going on inside you?

There's an energy. There's a certain . . . it just is. There's a mood. There's a presence. I think I create a feeling of intimacy, but at the same time excitement. I'm not consciously doing this stuff. I'm not thinking ahead to the next question *ever*, nor the last answer after he's answered it or she's answered it. I am in the moment, that moment. I listen totally to what the guest says. And then the next question shoots from me.

I have total confidence in myself; I'm in total control of the situation. Doesn't matter if I'm on home base or who I have on the show. And I have—there's no other way of putting it except—an innate curiosity. It never stops; it just never stops. You don't want to sit next to me on the airplane. I want to know who you are, what you do, why you do it.

I'm fascinated by the whole process. Not jaded. I don't know it all. I hate people who know it all. I never learned anything when I was talking. I have a lot of respect for people of accomplishment. That's important to me. I respect that somebody accomplishes something—whether it's publish a book, speak in public, try a case, legislate a law, govern a nation, anything. And I think that all rolls into one ball of wax.

The missing element that's unexplainable is "it's unexplainable." No one knows how to package that. It's a certain essence. I know it's intense and I know it's involved. It's a lot of things. But it's hard to self-examine.

Looking back at how much influence Larry King Live *had in the 1992 election, would you do anything differently?*

No. I've done what I've been doing for thirty-three years. The most interesting thing about 1992 was that what happened nationally, and indeed globally, with CNN was a regular form of life to me in the sixties and seventies in Miami. When I started doing talk in 1968, I had Humphrey on, and Nixon and Wallace—but it was all local. Jimmy Carter did a lot of talk shows in the Iowa primaries in '76. Reagan was a regular on talk shows in California.

What was the new phenomena was national talk in prime time—phone calls on television. We broke a lot of ground with that, and of course we were international. And then subsequently, we one night have Ross Perot on. Not unusual, he'd been on before, politicians had been on a lot, Bush had been on as vice president. We weren't doing anything differently than we always did. I asked good questions, I listened to the answers, I'd follow up on what's said. And that night with Perot, he mentioned that if he got on the ballot in all fifty states, and what happened was that people responded to him. And the rest is history.

Why do you think your show and other talk shows became so influential?

I think it was a question of timing; the times fit. It was the nineties; CNN is now in over 62 million homes. This wouldn't have been possible ten years ago; CNN wouldn't have been in that many homes—the impact CNN has and our show being on prime time and the fact that a lot of influential people watch it, follow up on it. The next day, after Perot said he would run, the first person to follow up on the Perot show was David Gergen. Gergen called and got a transcript and ran the story in *U.S. News and World Report* the next week.

Do you think people were getting fed up with "inside-the-beltway" journalism, so to speak?

In retrospect, yes. . . . I don't know if people were fed up, but I think there's just—there's a desire for more. I don't know that people would say, "Gee, I'm upset with this press conference." But I think there was a great desire for more and the best proof of that was the numbers that the debates got. The reason those debates did so well, so much viewership, is that those three people had become "Bill and George and Ross." We knew them from *Larry King Live* and from *Donahue* and from so many sources. And this was the first time we saw all three of them together, so naturally the audience was as big as a Superbowl audience. But it was all of our collective efforts that brought that about.

Do you think that because there were so many different ways to see the candidates, after a while we developed a more personal sense for the candidates?

Well, there are other advantages to talk shows other than the fullness of them. One, talk shows are much more diverse than a press conference. A press conference is all over the board; people don't follow up on questions. The president or whoever's running a press conference controls it.

If Larry King is interviewing Barry Goldwater tonight, if it's just me and him—you're not going to see every side of him, but, God, if you're watching for an hour solid of a political figure, and people are calling in, you can feel immediately that you can get in touch with them.

There's a great deal of personal aspect to it that can't occur on the Sunday morning shows or the press conferences. Because Bill Clinton's in your living room. And if you like him in your living room, and you hear a neighbor call from across the country in Phoenix and you're in San Antonio—you hear someone call and he responds—you know him. So what happens the next day is that the paper says, "Clinton didn't look good," and you thought he looked good, the paper's irrelevant. What they've done is, they've come right to you and there's nothing negative in that. I can't figure a negative.

Why should I need a newspaperman to be my middleman? I needed him when I didn't have a camera. I don't need him now. I don't mind the newspaper writer who says, "Bill Clinton is ineffective." I don't mind reading that. However, what's so important now is, it's almost moot to discuss it. The medium is so important, television's so relevant, that if you saw Clinton last night and liked him and he moved you, all the newspapers in the world couldn't change you today. You liked him. If you didn't like him, they're not going to get you to like him.

And the more we put people right in front of people, they're going to know people better. Now what happens from that is—it's not our fault, we're the presenter—is that if you're good, you're going to do well and if you're not, you're not going to do well.

What do you think of the view that Perot is a brilliant manipulator of the media—that he's cast himself as a "humble servant," yet he's been thinking about gaining political power, about a plan for a "United We Stand America" for a long time?

If Perot had a "master plan," then why did he quit the race in 1992? I mean, was that a master plan? The difficulty in Perot is not that he has a plan, but that he's impetuous. I think he quit that race in one minute. I think something bugged him; he hung up the phone, went out and talked to a press conference and quit. I think he was sorry the next day.

He's one of the best salesmen that ever lived. We respond to salesmen. I mean, here's a billionaire who sold himself as "Ross." He's not "Mr. Perot"; he's "Ross." He travels by himself, one driver, no entourage. Seems like a regular guy. Is a critic. Harps. Smart. He pulled back a little on the criticism of Clinton. That's smart. He's not stupid. What he does to the establishment is drive them bonkers.

Do you think he has the temperament to make a good president?

He said to me he didn't. In fact, that's the first thing he said to me back in February of 1992, "I don't have the temperament to be a good president." I would say that he has the temperament that could go either way. He could be terrible some days and fantastic others. He would be up and down. We would love him. There would be things he would do that we'd never see a president do. Less pomp, less circumstance. No balls. No high society . . . he's not pompous.

On the other hand he is impetuous. I would fear Ross hanging up the phone on the British prime minister. Getting mad and taking an action against Britain. There's some Truman in him. There's some Reagan in him . . . but whatever it is, he appeals to us. He is the first guy with no ax to grind. He don't need the money. He don't need the power. He don't need the job. His ego's enormously in it. But he's not beholden to either party. He doesn't need Ted Koppel or Larry King to like him—he can buy time.

One problem Perot had in 1992 is that experienced political handlers, such as Ed Rollins, found him very difficult to work with. Why do you think that was so?

He's very set in his own ways. He's had enormous success making decisions for himself. He doesn't like the word "handler." He doesn't like the word "let's strategize this"— that ain't his game. He has enormous self-confidence. So I think it would be almost impossible to handle him. David Gergen could do it. He has enormous respect for him. Gergen does not think he's the smartest person on earth and Gergen can give input without making it "I know everything."

When you look back at all the political figures you've interviewed, who had the least ego, the least "taste for power" and the most desire to make a difference?

Jimmy Carter didn't have a great ego. Carter has his life in balance. Pretty good head on him. Best former president we ever had. Cuomo didn't have that one extra step, that "I'm better than you and I can do the job." He had everything else. He had all the components of leadership—great character—he had vision but was unwilling to take that one extra step the candidate has to take.

And that step is?

"I can do this job." Hey, that's a large ego! Now it takes an ego to say, "I can be governor of New York." I have to have an ego to go on television every night. Probably the least "ego" person I ever interviewed in politics was Eleanor Roosevelt. I interviewed her when I was very young and just starting. She never used the word "I" . . . she was incredible. Enormous guts and moxie. But she didn't care if you loved her or hated her. Didn't care how she looked, but she had ideas about people. And she was *passionate* about things.

NOTES

1. Weisberg, Jacob, "White House Beast," *Vanity Fair*, September, 1993, p. 140.

2. King, Larry, with Joffe, Emily, *Larry King* (New York: Simon & Schuster, 1982), p. 8.

3. *Ibid.*, p. 29.

4

PIERRE SALINGER

Pierre Salinger served as Press Secretary to President
John F. Kennedy. He recently retired from his post as
ABC News' Senior Editor in Europe.

In 1958, as a Senate committee investigator, Pierre Salinger questioned a union official suspected of stealing union funds. There was one $240 check the official had written, Salinger told him, that was still a mystery. The official reached into his desk drawer, pulled out a gun, and pointed it at Salinger's head. "I used the money to buy this," the official said. His heart pounding, Salinger convinced the man to hand over the gun. Then he emptied the gun barrel and finished his questions.[1]

Salinger had been researching the underworld of Hoffa's powerful Teamsters Union as a journalist for *Collier's* magazine, when Robert Kennedy hired him in 1956 to be an investigator for his Senate Committee on Labor Racketeering. A year later, at a Senate hearing in Washington, Robert Kennedy tapped Salinger on the shoulder and said, "Pierre, I want you to meet my brother Jack."[2]

Salinger joined the inner circle of advisers who charted John Kennedy's victory in the 1960 presidential campaign. At the age of thirty-five, he began his term as JFK's press secretary, during perhaps one of the most idealistic periods of American politics. He endured horrible periods of grief and disillusionment after John Kennedy's, and then Robert Kennedy's, assassination—an anguish for Salinger which was deeply personal. Both had been close friends who had inspired him enormously.

While television did not play a big role in the 1960 campaign overall, 1960 was the campaign that put television on the map. Kennedy's success during the televised debates with Nixon transformed him from an unknown figure to a promising national candidate. After the election, Salinger suggested that Kennedy do a press conference live on television, which resulted in the first televised presidential press conference.

In 1993 Salinger retired from his post as ABC News' senior editor in Europe at the London Bureau. He had been with ABC News in many roles, as correspondent, bureau chief, and editor, for over ten years. He is one of the globe's top experts on terrorism, another underworld teeming with intrigue. It was a rocky path that led Salinger back to journalism and to a new life in Europe. After JFK's assassination, he was appointed to the U.S. Senate to serve out the term of the late Senator Claire Engle, but he lost the seat in the 1964 election. After working on George McGovern's unsuccessful 1972 presidential bid, Salinger moved to France and worked as a correspondent for *L'Express* and then began his work for ABC News. Salinger rose through the ranks at ABC, earning a reputation for breaking stories and getting behind-the-scenes information in his coverage of terrorist incidents such as the bombing of Pam Am Flight 103 and the Iran hostage crisis.

Salinger has co-authored two spy thrillers with Leonard Gross, drawing on his knowledge of terrorism and espionage. Glimpses of Salinger's character can be found in these novels. The protagonist of *Mortal Games*, André

Kohl, beats the odds in a corrupt world of international espionage and manages to cross the threshold into a new life. Waist-deep in deception and danger, Kohl still longs for a world "small enough so that everything in it could be genuine."[3]

After Kennedy was assassinated, Lyndon Johnson asked you to stay on as press secretary. Why did you leave?

Johnson had a different mentality about the press entirely. He wanted to manipulate. He called meetings every morning, about five or six people there, and said, "Alright, you attack this reporter. . . ." I had tried to resign after Kennedy died; Johnson wouldn't accept my resignation, because he was trying to have a transition that looked normal, trying to keep all the Kennedy people around him. I decided that I couldn't say "No" to him at that particular time, at that period of history. But at the same time I said, "I've got to figure a way to get out of the White House, but not make him mad at me by doing it."

When I left the White House, I said to myself—I didn't announce it publicly—that I would not return to journalism for ten years. Because I believed that someone who has been a spokesman for a president—who has adopted a political viewpoint while he's working for a president—he's not a credible journalist, if he doesn't stay out of journalism for a very solid period of time. There are some people who disagree with me, like Bill Moyers, for example, who had not even been a journalist until he became press secretary, and then immediately went into journalism afterwards and has been a journalist ever since.

When you're in the explosive business of news coverage, you are surrounded by all kinds of efforts at disinformation, all kinds of efforts at manipulation. And sometimes you want to get out of it and do something else, except that I think any reputable journalist, knowing that these things are going on, is going to fight against it, try to overcome those efforts of people to manipulate.

Many think that Ross Perot is a brilliant manipulator of the media in that he casts himself as a "reluctant and humble" candidate and yet many point out that his organization, United We Stand America, is very much run top-down, not bottom-up, and that Perot has harbored political aspirations for years.

I think that's true. Perot went further than the other candidates in terms that he was buying hours and half-hours on shows and doing it himself. I mean, he was not being interrogated; he was just putting on his own show, putting on his own points. It's somewhat different if you go on the air and you're being questioned.

But Perot was also the representative of American frustration with the political system in 1992. Ross Perot knew that there were a very large number of Americans who didn't like the Republicans or the Democrats. And so he decided to put himself on the table, thinking that it was possible to win. And then he made a dramatic mistake when he pulled out during the Democratic convention in July. Because I'm absolutely convinced that if he'd stayed in the race all the way through, that he would have gotten even more of the vote than he did.

What do you think of the charge that Reagan's handlers had so much success in manipulating network journalists because journalists were under so much pressure to get better ratings and Reagan's handlers provided them with the photo-ops and one-liners that would supposedly help them get better ratings?

Well, we've always been under pressure to get better ratings. And there's always been a struggle between the evening news shows to see which one is the best, no question, in terms of audience. But I think it's an absolute joke to say that we handled Reagan in order to help our ratings situation. I mean, that is a joke.

There's a conservative media group, which puts out a weekly bulletin showing how the media are leftists. And they attack the media constantly for things they say about Ronald Reagan . . . being "critical, unfair." . . . Was the media easy on him in the Iran-contra affair? Not at all.

The way Reagan handled himself with the media was quite good. But Reagan himself had this impressive power of talking to the people, which we've not seen in the United States since John Kennedy was president. I mean, he really had the ability to speak on television in a very convincing way. He was entirely different than Kennedy in his approach to the press. He created a new form of journalism, which I call shouting journalism, because he was inaccessible. He was not a guy that would see journalists.

But in the long run I think the press covered Reagan in a very honest way. And were not totally taken in by the way he did it. I don't agree with those people who think that the press totally was eating the dessert that Reagan was putting on the floor for them like little dogs. I think that we covered Reagan in a very honest, direct way. And sometimes we found what he did was positive and sometimes what we found was negative. In the eight years of the Reagan presidency I've made many, many comments on Reagan and sometimes I would say some positive things and sometimes I would say negative things. It depended on how it looked.

A former producer of CBS News was quoted as saying that Mike Deaver, one of Reagan's aides, was so deft at manipulating the media that he should have been listed as the executive producer for some of the newscasts. What do you think of that remark?

Well I think that's outrageous. When Reagan made his first trip to Europe, Michael Deaver came over here a month before the trip and had lunch with me. He knew I had a Democratic background, but he also knew I'd been living in Europe for twenty years and I knew this part of the world better than their people did. And he said, "What is our problem in Europe and what do we do to correct that problem?"

The main problem at the time the Reagan administration started was that they were not disseminating their own information in Europe with the same quality the Soviets were. I don't take credit for it, but I'm sure it had an influence on it—the creation of WorldNet, this television network that USIA created where they did press conferences with important American officials, but with European correspondents asking questions by satellite. That had a very major effect in Europe in helping the United States and, of course, the Reagan administration, spread its influence.

Reagan was not seen as a potentially good president of the United States here in Europe. I mean, the people just couldn't believe that the United States had elected a man like Ronald Reagan president. And yet at the end of his first term, there were a series of polls in European countries which showed that if he had run in any one of these European countries he would have been elected by a wider majority than he was in the United States.

In other words, in four years his image in Europe had developed very, very strongly because of some of these things they were doing. For example, I said to Deaver, "If you really want to get some influence in Europe, here's what you do: You put together an interview for Ronald Reagan. And you invite four top journalists from four different European countries, European television channels, and let them interview him together, in a kind of round-table discussion with Reagan. It'll carry on British, German, French, Italian television. It'll be very useful." They did it. But that doesn't make Deaver the Executive Producer; it's just an idea that is put into effect. And, believe me, some of the executive producers of our shows are very, very liberal Democrats. Jeff Gralnick, who is now at NBC, did our specials and was very much involved in presidential coverage—he worked in the campaign of George McGovern.

The interview in 1988 when Bush and Rather fought live on the air during a CBS News broadcast is often cited as an attempt by Rather to improve his ratings. What did you think was going on when you watched it?

It just happened I was living in Europe at that time, and I turned on the morning news in Paris and the first story was about this interview that Rather had done. In Paris we can watch Dan Rather's show at eight o'clock in the morning. So I watched it and I was absolutely shocked by the way he dealt with Bush in that interview. He was just trying to provoke an uproar to give himself some kind of image as a tough guy. . . . I mean, I don't shout at people. There are ways of getting information where you don't have to shout at people.

But it benefited Bush?

I think in the long run it did. Yes.

Do you think it was staged by Bush advisers?

No . . . I think it was Rather's game. Rather's big problem right now is he's sunk to Number Three in the United States; he's no longer even Number Two. And CBS is in a period of concern about whether they want to keep Rather or not. He's done some fakes too. He did this whole thing in Afghanistan which was a total fake. They gave the impression that he was really doing reporting in Afghanistan, and smuggled him in for two hours for a stand-up and that was it.

Many critics blame television news for obsessing on character issues, and they say that it's trivializing presidential campaigns. Is there any truth to that?

I don't think it's a media issue; I think it's a political issue. I think that the parties have got to restructure the system so they regain their power to play a major role in the selection of presidential candidates and the only way they can do that is by suppressing primaries. If you suppress primaries I think that there will be much less focus on personalities than there will be on issues.

When John Kennedy ran for president in 1960, except for the television debates between him and Nixon, television was a very small item. Television was just getting started really, in an important way. The evening news shows were fifteen minutes. What those shows did was not our major concern at that time. Our major concern was major newspapers, wire services, magazines, not television.

But the election process was entirely different then; the party had total control over the selection process. In 1960 there were something like sixteen primaries in the United States, which meant that in the other thirty-four states of the union the delegates were chosen by party conventions or they were chosen by party bosses, in smoke-filled rooms, but the party had total control over the selection process.

In 1972 they changed the process; they expanded the number of primaries across the country. And by doing so, they took away from the party any power over the selection process. And the most important thing to understand if you're looking at television as a major factor, is what you're looking at in the campaign moved from issues to personalities. It became a personality issue because people had to run all over the country, trying to win primaries. It developed into making people presidential candidates that never would have been presidential candidates under the old system; it obviously thrust the media into a different context, in looking at political campaigns.

And it developed among other things this whole new "search" for all the "secrets" of a candidate—"What kind of a life does he lead? Does he have relations with women other than his wife? Is he a drunk? Has he done something monetarily that is illegal or can cause him to be thrown out of the race?" I mean, those things have become the focus of the election campaign now, and not the issues.

And it is not the media who invented that idea, but the media who obviously has adapted to what the political parties did to themselves by changing the system. Carter emerges out of the Iowa Caucus, which I consider ridiculous. The number of people voting is not significant and yet it puts you on the front—it puts you on the cover of *Time* and *Newsweek*, and the head of the list of all the television broadcasts and everything else, and it suddenly makes you a national figure, since you got five thousand votes. Now many people today are arguing that we should go back to the old system, give the parties back the power. And if we ever did that you would also see a very massive change in how the media covered the campaigns.

I mean, many people today spend a lot of time talking about John Kennedy and his girlfriends—that was not an issue in 1960. No one ever brought it up as an issue in 1960. I think in the whole time I was press secretary I got one person—came and asked me a question. "There're rumors that the president's having girlfriends." . . . And I said "Listen. The President works from eight o'clock in the morning until eleven o'clock at night; he's running this country; if he's got time to have an affair with another girl, I think that's not a problem at all." And the guy walked out.

Tell me, are you ever going to ever find anybody running for president who didn't do something bad in his life? Anybody? I don't like the coverage of the campaigns at all, but, at the same time I understand that covering the campaigns becomes more and more difficult.

In the 1992 campaign the American people seemed to be turning away from the idea of "personal life." If you remember debate number three between Bush and Clinton, which was the only one where the public asked questions, right at the beginning of the debate somebody got up and said, "We're not going to discuss personal lives— that's not an issue in this campaign. We want to know what these candidates are going to do and how they are going to run this country." And I think that there was a roundabout feeling in America that maybe all this stuff about private lives was moving people away from knowledge on what the candidates were capable of doing.

There was a lot of private-life stuff in the 1992 campaign. The kind of stuff that was blown on Clinton early in the primaries made a lot of people feel that he would never make it to the nomination. How he turned that around was absolutely spectacular. Because if it had been in the same mentality political environment as when Gary Hart ran eight years before, Clinton probably wouldn't have made it to the nomination.

If you could change the primary system, what would you do?

I would eliminate the system completely as it exists today. I just think it's a terrible system. I would give the power back to the party. I'd eliminate most of the primaries—go back to just a number of primaries. You could put them across the country in different states so you'd have some idea on regions, but not primaries in every state. Bring back state conventions that would select delegates from those states. I would eliminate advertising—no advertis-

ing on television or radio, because I think that the advertising has been turned into strictly negative advertising,
and I don't think that that is a useful way of running a
campaign either. And then I would change the whole
system of the debates. I would put in the European debate,
where the two candidates sit opposite each other and
debate each other. And you don't have journalists asking
the question; you have a mediator who maybe will say
three or four times during that one hour or two hours that
they're opposite—"Well, we've been talking now about
foreign policy for an hour; why don't we talk now about
domestic policy." Those kind of debates, where you're really going to have discussions of subjects.

*Didn't Americans' experience with Nixon during Water-
gate also fuel the concern over character we now see in
campaigns?*

Well, Nixon was a double personality—Nixon is a double
personality. One side he has this weird view of life, all
about Watergate. On the other hand he was very, very good
in foreign policy. He was an excellent foreign policy president. He was the president since Kennedy who moved
towards some kind of understanding with the Soviet Union. He was the one who opened relations with China. You
know, he did some very, very positive things in his foreign
policy. The only surprise that Watergate caused me was
his not going on the air like twenty-four hours later and
saying, "This is my fault. I've made a mistake and I'm
getting rid of these guys. They never asked me about this
and I don't approve of this kind of thing and so on." And
that would have been the end of Watergate.

Certainly it's had an effect on the relationship between
the press and the White House. There's a conflict going on
all the time which didn't exist before. In the days when I
was Press Secretary, there was respect between the White
House and the press. We had no confrontational situ-

ations. Of course, we were much more open to the press at that time than we recently have been. I held two briefings a day; they only hold one briefing a day now. The president had a press conference at least once every two weeks, sometimes more often. Watergate and Vietnam, both of those had an effect of changing the relationship of the press and the White House. All this talk about the fact that the press was kind of part of the White House operation is just so wrong, because of this whole new mood that they adopted after the Watergate. And part of it was that a lot of young journalists, who had seen Woodward and Bernstein become famous by having carried this out, they decided—"There must be something out there that I can find that will make me just as famous."

Are there any presidential candidates who you feel were unfairly destroyed by the media?

There've been some candidates who've been destroyed by the media—but they have also played a role in destroying themselves. Gary Hart is an example of that. I mean, Gary Hart, in my opinion, would have been a very intelligent president, much more powerful Democratic candidate than Michael Dukakis. But from the start one of the reasons why the media got quite excited about him was that he had changed his name. His name wasn't "Hart." He had changed his age; he gave a false age. Made himself younger. And those facts emerged. And, you know, those kind of facts are the kind of facts that do make the media pounce on somebody, saying, you know, "If they do that, maybe there's something else behind them that we don't know about." His real name was "Hartpence."

And then, of course, when the story of womanization came up, he was stupid enough to make the statement "Listen, if you think I'm screwing around with ladies, follow me around." So they did and they found him. Right. I mean, you have to have a certain discretion. If you're going to do that and you're running for president, you have to be discreet, right? I think the person has got to be judged on his ability, his political ability, his overall knowledge to be a good president of the United States. And not on whether he's had a girlfriend.

What do you say to the view that it's the fault of broadcast journalists that sound bites wield so much power in campaigns?

Well, that's gotten to be a big issue—"Now we used to have forty-second sound bites; now we have eight-second sound bites." That's not dealing with reality. I mean, day after day a president of the United States says anything, he goes live, he says everything, right on camera. And then you have twenty people come on and comment about it. We're not in the sound-bite world anymore. With live television, which has become *the* factor, anytime anything important happens we go live. We interrupt entertainment; we go live. Obviously if you're being interviewed for *World News Tonight*, you know that it's intelligent to make a short statement.

I think it's unfair to say that the networks don't look at issues anymore. I mean, you cannot just focus on the evening news broadcasts, because we do so many other things. During the 1988 campaign, for example, our *Nightline* show, which is an issue show, concentrated on the issues of the campaigns by having people speak about—from different viewpoints—about those issues. The *MacNeil/Lehrer Report* focuses on issues in campaigns; *The Brinkley Show* focuses on issues in campaigns, not on personalities. So there's a lot of television news which is focusing on issues.

But after almost thirty years of writing journalism, when I went into television journalism for the first time in 1978, I had the most frustrating year and a half of my entire journalistic career. On the one hand, I was used to writing three-thousand words on a major subject, and then you have the same subject and you do a one-minute, forty-five-second piece—it's extremely frustrating for a journalist. And I don't think I would have stayed in television unless I had run into a situation where I was allowed to work one year on a story—a three-hour documentary, *America Held Hostage*. And that is really what launched me into this business.

I've done a lot of these long things, and those things really make you feel like you're making a journalistic contribution. I do a lot of things for *Nightline*. Last year, this very time of year, I was in Moscow at the very special meeting of ten Americans, ten Cubans, ten Russians, all of whom had participated in the Cuban Missile Crisis, sitting around a table for three days and discussing it. Well *Nightline* gave me an hour to discuss it.

There was a lot of criticism of how the networks covered the 1988 campaign. Do you think that there were efforts towards reform on the part of the networks?

I think that the networks were much better in the '92 election than they have been for a long time. I think that they were much more open to the candidates in letting them take questions and speak a long time. You look at our network, *Good Morning America* spent hours and hours and hours interviewing the candidates, they were all appearing on *Nightline*, they were appearing on *Larry King Live* and a lot of other shows. It was a much wider look at what the candidates had to say and how they were saying it and their positions on a number of important issues.

The image of Kennedy, his "mystique," is so strong and there are also so many sensationalistic stories about him. How do you compare all that to the man you knew?

Well, I don't agree with the word "mystique" or the word "Camelot"—I think that he was a human being. I don't believe in looking back on Kennedy in some mythical way. I think you have to look at what Kennedy did in fact. He did some things that were very, very good, and he did some things that were bad. But he was a president who was not looking at the country on a day-to-day basis, and trying to solve today's problems today, and tomorrow's problems tomorrow. He was looking ahead twenty, thirty, forty years—where are we going to guide this country? And that was the great strength that he had, that he was looking at America in the future as well as the present. Very, very important. And Americans felt that they were part of the operation. The White House was not one place and them somewhere else. They were part of the White House.

NOTES

1. Salinger, Pierre, *With Kennedy* (New York: Doubleday & Company, 1966), p. 25.

2. *Ibid.*, p. 20.

3. Salinger, Pierre, and Gross, Leonard, *Mortal Games* (New York: St. Martin's Press, 1988), p. 15.

5

DAVE SIRULNICK

Dave Sirulnick is the Director of MTV News.

When Dave Sirulnick arrived, the small eight-by-twelve-foot holding room was crammed with almost a dozen people. Three cars behind President Bush's private car on the campaign train, the holding room was where aides waited to see the president. MTV correspondent Tabitha Soren had waited there while Sirulnick and his camera crew covered the president's stump speech at the last train stop. When Sirulnick came in, they shuffled their equipment to make more space. In the room, along with several Secret Service escorts, were National Security Council Chief Brent Scowcroft, Campaign Director James Baker, and presidential aides Mary Matalin and Tory Clark. Sirulnick exchanged a few awkward greetings with them and then squatted next to Tabitha Soren, who was waiting for their interview with the president.

The atmosphere was dour and tense—three days before Election Day in 1992, the polls showed slim hope for a Bush victory. Sirulnick and Soren were filled with uneasy anticipation. Until that day the Bush campaign had refused them any access to the campaign. "I'm not going to be a teeny-bopper at sixty-eight,"[1] Bush had quipped, when asked if he'd appear on MTV, a remark which nagged him for the rest of the campaign. As MTV News gained more credibility and recognition, the pressure on Bush to appear on MTV increased. Grudgingly, the Bush campaign granted them an interview just before Election Day. So when Press Secretary Tory Clark told Sirulnick they'd do the interview in just a few minutes, Sirulnick thought, "Good! Let's get on with it."

Ten years before Sirulnick would hardly have predicted that in 1992 he'd find himself crammed in a holding room with presidential aides and a camera crew. In 1982 Sirulnick was studying theater at Rutgers University and booking rap artists in the New York metropolitan area. Rap music was just taking hold and Sirulnick was very successful at placing the new, controversial musicians in clubs in New Jersey and New York.

After graduating from Rutgers, Sirulnick went to work for CNN. Sirulnick had spent his summers as a teenager in TV studios watching his father, a television producer, at work. So when Sirulnick arrived at CNN, he'd already dipped a toe in both television and the music business. Sirulnick moved up the ranks and became the music producer for CNN's *Show Biz Today*, covering rock 'n' roll, jazz, and pop events. In 1987 MTV courted Sirulnick to produce their new newscast, *The Week in Rock*.

What might have been a hodgepodge of talents in other circumstances was a perfect mix for the new director of MTV News—Sirulnick had a quick instinct for how to combine music and television production and for how young people relate to politics. The news operation gradually incorporated more stories on politics and social issues. After concluding their Gulf War coverage in 1991, the producers set their sights on 1992. Impressed by the low voter turnout among its young audience, the news division launched its "Choose or Lose" campaign coverage for 1992, which included daily reports on the campaign and Q & A forums with candidates. The goal was to get young voters more engaged in politics and to do it through their language—the rhythmic, unpredictable, video parlance of MTV.

"The MTV generation" is part of every media critic's vocabulary. MTV is often cast as television's "wicked trendsetter of the eighties," the symbolic embodiment of everything that's wrong with television. The preference for fast-cut stories, the refinement of visual seduction for commercial purposes, the blurring of the lines between advertising and programming are all trends which are associated with MTV and criticized as having made television news programming less substantive and more prone to manipulation by political handlers.

But for others, especially young Americans, MTV's programming is often a mirror of their sense of themselves and their world. Its visual style communicates to them in ways that more traditional broadcasting has never been able to do. By combining the power of music and the visual potency of television, MTV has created a cultural medium of enormous influence.

During the 1984 campaign, MTV periodically flashed a picture of Ronald Reagan on the screen along with the question "Does this man like MTV?" Lee Atwater, then campaign strategist to President Reagan, had requested a copy of a music video to show Reagan, and MTV didn't let the request go unnoticed.[2] Atwater understood that the music video had created a new youth culture, and that in 1984 this culture remained politically untapped.

It wasn't until 1992 that a presidential candidate would pick up where Atwater left off and court the youth vote through MTV. Bill Clinton's first MTV forum was a turning point for his campaign, which showcased his flair for spontaneous give-and-take with an audience. But it's not unimaginable that the likes of Lee Atwater and an equally talented Republican candidate could successfully court young voters through MTV. MTV viewers are hardly an updated version of the revolutionary generation of the sixties. They are mainly white, suburban youth who are economically conservative and socially liberal.

President Bush and Vice President Quayle both turned down requests from MTV to host similar forums, and their absence from the screen added to the appearance of lopsided coverage in favor of Clinton. As the 1992 campaign progressed, it became clear why the Clinton campaign was so quick to give access to "the music network." MTV's numbers were formidable. The newscasts reached 2 million young voters weekly. Of the political specials MTV ran that year, some attracted as many as 8 million viewers. And in a postelection poll of eighteen- to twenty-nine-year-olds, 12 percent said that MTV's coverage directly influenced their vote. From that age group, 22 million voted in 1992. Clinton won by 5.5 million votes.[3] "We made sure we made time for MTV. We wouldn't replace Jennings for Soren, but it was close," said Ginny Terzano, a senior Democratic press official during the campaign.[4]

Like most national media, MTV News received criticism for a bias in favor of Clinton in '92. But if MTV News was biased, it's more likely that bias resulted from a vigilant pursuit of its audience's interests than of a specific political agenda. MTV's success is in part due to its mastery of "niche marketing," the tailoring of its programming to a specific audience. "MTV is only biased in its story selection," says media critic Jon Katz. "I don't think it has any real political agenda. I think they're basically saying, 'This is what younger people, college kids, are really interested in, so we're going to cover these stories.'" And those stories are about issues such as abortion, AIDS, education, the environment, jobs, and racism.

Like *The New Yorker* or *The National Review*, MTV News speaks to a specific audience, in part reflecting, in part influencing, its views. Judged on the basis of its ability to express points of view, MTV News offered refreshingly irreverent coverage in 1992. The lack of decorum, unusual camera angles, and tight, rhythmic editing all made for unconventional coverage without being sensationalistic. What started out as a small, offbeat news operation succeeded in reaching scores of young people and getting the message out that, as far as politics goes, it's hip to be involved.

How did MTV News get started?

Well, we originally did issues mostly relating to rock and roll and pop culture. And we decided slowly but surely that we didn't need to just cover rock and roll, that our audience was interested in a lot of other issues, whether it was the environment, an abortion issue, a sexism issue, or a racism issue.

So we slowly started making headway into that and had reasonable success with it, on our own terms. At the same time each year we were doing *The Year in Rock*, which would put in perspective a lot of the year's events, and we felt that we were to a degree forging a new style of news presentation. It crystallized itself at the end of 1989 when we did a program called *Decade*, which was a look back at the eighties. It was a two-hour program and it was a shining example of this new style that we had been working with for about a year or so.

And when the Gulf War came about in 1991, we felt, we've got to cover this—this is our audience who's fighting, who have friends or relatives that are fighting, people who they know and it's going to affect them. This was really the first full scale war that was going to affect the MTV generation so directly. So we took this same style that we had felt comfortable with and applied it to various issues surrounding the war. So when 1992 came around it wasn't like we just woke up one day and said, "You know what? All we've been doing is covering concerts, now let's cover the campaign!"

What were you most concerned with when you were designing your coverage?

The idea that we set out with was "Let's explain, let's demystify this entire process that this country goes through every four years." One thing that was very important to us from the start was that we knew we were not going to be a competitor to CNN or ABC or any of the other television networks. Our approach was, "If you want to know all the details, if you want to know everything that's going on, you've got to be well informed yourself, you've got to read newspapers and watch other media. If you just watch us, you'll get some of it. If you watch us, hopefully you'll see why these things are important to you, or should be important to you." We don't feel like we're competing with the networks. And just within MTV, Tabitha is not competing with another reporter for air time. She's talking to a very focused, narrow audience, while your network newscaster is talking to "everybody," or supposedly "everybody."

We'd cover some things, some things we wouldn't. We knew that we were not the be-all and end-all of coverage. We simply knew that eighteen- to twenty-four-year-olds were the audience we had decided to focus on. Those were the ones who had voted in such low numbers in '88 and also in '84. We also knew that the eighteen- to twenty-four-year-olds that we're talking about don't watch *Mac-Neil/Lehrer,* don't watch Peter Jennings or CNN regularly, don't get their news from those kinds of sources. And so we said, "We can do something about this!" Not so much that we can get them to vote, but if we interest them, excite them about the political process and educate them about it—we knew that they would become self-starters and go out there and do something.

And of course we came up with the name "Choose or Lose," which really means, we want young people to choose a candidate, to take a stand, take an interest in your future or you're losing out. You can't bitch and moan about who's president if you didn't vote. You can't say things are going bad in this country and things are going wrong if you don't choose to stand up and do something about it. That title was a call to action as well as being a title for our coverage. It really galvanized what we wanted to do.

We knew that no one else was talking directly to this young group, and we in the news department felt—we've got a really great opportunity. We're going to talk to a real specific group, we're going to talk to them in the way we know how to reach them—we're going to speak their language.

How did this translate into the style of your newscasts?

Well, our coverage has always tried to be, We know you couldn't make it to this cool concert, we know you couldn't make it to the debate, you couldn't make it to the convention. We're going to take you there. We're going to try and show you the way we saw it. We have a very close relationship with our audience. We are very similar in age and in style and the way we like to see things. I mean, all of us were struck by how the conventions are just like giant rock festivals [laughing], as far as all the credentials and the media, the important players . . . the T-shirt sales and all the merchandise!

We wanted to try to break down those walls that sometimes occur when a reporter is standing outside an event and goes, "I'm here at the concert behind me," which creates an artificial wall, that this person is there, you're not. Most of the time when you would see Tabitha Soren out in the field being our reporter, she was not doing what the networks would call a traditional stand-up when you saw her on camera. Generally speaking, she was not just standing still outside the White House, outside the Capitol, you know, the traditional shot. We would try to find different places and angles to shoot from. If she was out there wearing jeans, that was fine. That was the audience she was talking to. They were going to accept her; there wasn't any reason she couldn't be wearing something like that . . . it's a hot, sunny day, we're in the middle of Manhattan in July, why can't she wear sunglasses outside? You know, why not? That's what our audience would do.

When we were covering the candidates up in New Hampshire during the primary, you'd see a lot of shots of Tabitha with the candidates. And what that did for our audience right away was show "OK, here are some candidates. They're willing to talk to a young girl who's twenty-four. Who's asking them serious questions and who's asking questions for us, like 'What are you going to do about the job market for highly skilled college graduates who can't find a job?' " When young people saw Tabitha doing that, and saw these candidates up in New Hampshire giving her the time of day and taking her seriously, that was very effective and it really kickstarted our whole "Choose or Lose" campaign.

We wanted to get young people excited. If we put our coverage on in a bland format, people would have picked up their remotes and turned the channel, even if it was MTV. What I always talked to producers about is pacing. It doesn't mean "fast-paced"; it means *pacing*, that it's moving along. Is the story being told in an interesting way, in a way that's keeping your attention? Don't do this straight and bland. Everybody knows politics is straight and bland. Let's squeeze it and get the juice out of it.

Well, a criticism that we did receive of this was, "Well, you're unnecessarily making something that's not sexy, sexy." And we'd say, "Yes. We are. Thank you very much." Why not? Why sit there in the blandest way and explain something when you could do it in a much more fun, funky way? If the message is just as clear, if the ideas are clear, if the journalistic integrity is still sound, why not present it in a way that's going to be a lot hipper, a lot more fun to watch for our audience than in a straight, bland way? And I am no way going to say that the audience of CBS's *Evening News with Dan Rather* would have liked any of the pieces we did. They're attempting to reach too broad an audience that they can take a chance on that. We, on the other hand, aren't.

If people over the age of forty start tuning out, saying, "Achh, there's too many graphics! There's too much going on!"—well, guess what? Your sons and daughters who are twenty years old, who were raised on video games, and raised on MTV, they can grasp all that. People would say to us, "Well, it's just too fast!" It's not fast; it's well-paced. When we would do a bio about Jerry Brown or Clinton or Ross Perot or George Bush, we would spend four minutes on that piece. That's a good healthy chunk of time in television news package time, probably two and a half times the average length of a network news piece.

What do you say to criticism that Clinton got much more MTV News coverage than Bush did?

Well, we asked Bush to come on MTV, or even just be on his campaign bus, train, or whatever his mode of transportation was [laughing] throughout the entire campaign. And his press office kept turning us down. And we're talking back from January, throughout the whole campaign.

We'd ask, "We understand the president is going to be at such and such university making a speech in New

Jersey. We'd like press credentials, we'd like to be there, we'd like to cover it." They'd take down our information and we'd never hear back from them. And we'd call them, and call them and "Can we get there? Can we get there?" and they'd say, "Well you know it's too late. We've closed out the press; you know, we're filled." That is what would continually happen. We had access to and we were at the debates, until the Republican Convention, of course. But when we specifically had to get credentials from the Bush campaign we were just not a priority. We weren't thought of. And we continually asked, "Let us come out with you." And we just kept pushing, kept pushing. And that last weekend of the year, the Halloween weekend right before the election was when we finally got to do the interview with Bush.

All year long the voters saw what Clinton had done, not only with MTV, but in general, how many times he directly addressed young people's questions. Al Gore—we had done an hour and a half forum with him. Ross Perot, while he hadn't talked to us up until just before Election Day, every one of his speeches, every one of his messages was "The future, young people, we've got to reduce the deficit." So young people had an idea of what Perot meant. But I don't think Bush had ever really effectively communicated his message to young people. And this MTV interview was really an opportunity.

As far as MTV embracing the guy "who got it"—he got it himself, as far as Clinton understanding how to get his message across to people on MTV. Ross Perot got it just as well as Clinton. Here's a short, thin, wiry, older Texan, and this guy connected with more young people probably better than even Clinton did, because of his brash tone, his "Who the hell's running this country anyway?" kind of attitude. When we did an interview with him, he came across as "What a hoot! That old maverick!"

How did the interview with Bush go?

Well, if you remember from the shot, he was holding onto a little bar overhead, he had a doughnut in his hand and a cup of coffee. It was extremely noisy—the wind was blowing all over the place. We had the normal clackity clack of the train. Bush was splitting his time between looking at Tabitha and waving to any supporters who had come out to line the railroad tracks . . . and these were the conditions in which we were supposed to do our only interview with the president?

But we didn't have a lot of choice, so Tabitha got going and she asked serious questions—"Do you feel that you wrote off the young voter by saying that MTV is a teeny-bopper network? How is it fair that an average couple, making 53,000 dollars, were paying a certain percent in taxes, and yourself and Barbara, your taxable income was over a million dollars and you paid a lot lower percentage? How is that fair?"

He answered her questions, but the attitude, that any-body who has seen that tape, and the attitude that I got from standing right there, was that he didn't want to do it. I was standing there watching, and I think he looked at me, off camera, as many times as he looked at Tabitha. And the look in his eyes, when our eyes would meet, was one of "This is not something I want to be doing right now. I don't want to be doing this." That somewhere, somebody convinced him that this is something he needed to do that final weekend.

But when we went back into the car after the interview, the president's attitude'd changed—going from somebody who didn't want to be there, who seemed like he didn't want to be talking to us. All of a sudden it changed into the nice-guy attitude. All of a sudden he was shmoozing us! "How you guys doing? Where'd you come from? Are you staying on the train the whole way?" He said to Tabitha,

"Oh hey, let me show you something." He took her back out onto the little platform. "Let me show you how this is rigged up," he said. "Watch this. I got a little button here." And he hit the button and two microphones went on and he said, "Hey, thank you for coming out!" to the next little crowd that passed by.

So all of a sudden he'd become . . . full of life. We had an MTV baseball hat for him and he said, "Oh! You guys like baseball?" "Oh, yeah, I'm a big baseball fan." I said, "Yeah, you know, I saw you throw out a first pitch at a Mets game." And we're talking baseball. . . . It was just very interesting to see how he changed at the snap of a finger. How he just as soon as the camera stopped rolling, he became much more charming—you know, he was talking to the crew, "Oh! How're you guys doing?" and that kind of thing. The White House photographer snapped a couple of photos of us standing there with him. It was, "Well, hey, good luck with what you're doing!"

As far as I was concerned, when he was on camera a bad attitude was showing. It looked like someone's father "scolding" his young teenage daughter—Tabitha's not a teenager, but that's what it looked like. He wouldn't look her in the eye, and he was being very dismissive, almost like, "What you're talking about is not important" . . . very odd. And I think the body language and the attitude came through loud and clear.

And I think it backfired on the Bush campaign. They really had a chance to show young people that Bush was taking them seriously. I think that's the overriding thing that young voters were looking for. That here is the president of the United States, that he's interested in young people. And I think the body language, his terse answers, the content of his answers, showed a lot of people that he was being dismissive of the youth vote. And, when we got back inside the little car, that's when he changed.

The more presidential side and the more caring person came out at the wrong time as far as his campaign went. It wasn't until afterwards that I realized it seemed like the campaign was drawing some of the life out of him. He really seemed to me to be somebody who was somewhat desperate, somewhat unsure at that point. He had the look and the feel of somebody who knew "it had slipped away." And as soon as the cameras weren't rolling, and he didn't have to answer questions, he could be himself. He seemed to get the life back into him. From the few minutes that I saw, the off-camera time was when he was still a vibrant person.

And it seemed like he didn't quite understand . . . "Why do I have to talk to these people?" He's the president of the United States—why does he have to stand here and talk to MTV? This music channel, this rock and roll thing? It's ironic, because when we were at the Republican Convention, we interviewed a lot of different Republicans; we interviewed Newt Gingrich; we interviewed . . . Bush's son, Jeb Bush, and Mary Matalin and Rich Bond. And, both on camera and off camera, we asked them, "Do you think it's a good idea for the president of the United States, George Bush, to talk to MTV?" We asked Rich Bond, "Do you think it's a good idea for him to use the MTV News format to address young people's concerns?" And every one of them said, "Yes!"

Now, of course, they're on television, so they may want to say the right thing. But off camera Newt Gingrich was going on about how he watches MTV, and he watches MTV News. Right before the convention we had done two profiles of George Bush, and Gingrich came up to us unprompted, when we first met him at the convention, and said to us, "Those two pieces you did on the president last weekend were the two best pieces, fair and balanced pieces, I've seen on the president this year."

Whether somebody else had told him to try and schmooze us, we don't know, but it certainly seemed sincere. And when he was talking to us both on and off camera about trying to convince the president to go on MTV, how he thought that was a good move—he *got* it, he knew what MTV was about, he understood who was watching, he understood what was happening in 1992 with politics and with the presidential campaign.

Right-wing publications, columnists, radio talk-show personalities would try to hammer away at our coverage, saying that we're not giving Bush equal time. And when we did answer them, what we would say is, "We're trying! We're trying!" Dan Quayle wouldn't come either. We were asking these guys every week, and they wouldn't come on. And so for your average viewer who doesn't know that, it certainly had the appearance of, "Hey, how come we haven't seen them?" We started saying consistently, everytime you'd see Clinton, "We've asked the president and the vice president to come on."

And how did the Clinton campaign treat you?

They were very open to us. The exact opposite of Bush. They understood what we were about. They gave us access. They watched the pieces that we had done. They knew that college kids, young people, that the MTV audience was going to be important to his campaign. Whether from the moment Clinton decided to run for president he really had decided that he was going to go for this Kennedyesque appeal, or whether that came later in focus groups and with his strategy people, they knew when we got involved that young people would be an important part of this. And that here's MTV with an audience of millions of young people, targeted to young people, that young people tune in to hear what's going on. And they said, "Well, they're just as legitimate as anybody else."

What were your impressions of Clinton on camera and off camera during the first MTV forum with him?

Well, he was so at ease and so comfortable, it seemed that he was so in his element. During what would be commercial breaks he kept going. He would go out and walk into the audience and sit with them and talk with them. He would go back to people and say, "Hey that was a great question you asked!" Now maybe when he's in the limo getting there he's a different person. But my experience with him that day, prior to that, and since that day, I've always seen the same personality presented to myself and us at MTV. When it was over, again, he stayed there, he signed autographs, he took photos with people—he kept talking to people. You could see that he was having a great time.

And as we went through the show, the questions were not easy. The questions were hard hitting. There was a girl who questioned him about his abortion stand, "How do you think there should be parental notification? I think that's absurd! What about an abusive parent; how could you expect a child to go tell a parent that?" Confronting him, just like that. Not any reverential "This is a potential president, hey, we gotta be nice. . . ." There was a young black kid who was like seventeen or eighteen; he said, "What are you going to do that's going to show me, my friends, my community, that there's any hope. That anybody cares about us?"

And something to Bill Clinton's credit that we saw in that show and that we've seen since, was that he likes the give and take. He does not shy away. When the girl asked him about abortion, he said, "I understand, that's your opinion, that's your side of it. OK, now listen to my side of it. I'm going to give you my reasons for my side of it. And if you don't completely agree with me, OK, but let me tell you."

And I think with Tabitha and President Bush, the physical nature of the way Bush presented himself, the body language, the attitude—Bill Clinton with this audience was showing people he respected them. He was listening to them; he was looking directly at them. Whether it was an act or not, and I don't think it was, he came off as a guy who cares about young people and a guy who's passionate about the issues. He was not being dismissive, and he knew that these people were important, that these people were the future. And more people called me and told me that they thought Bill Clinton in that forum came off the best that he had been up until that point in the campaign—that it showed him off the best. He took the opportunity and ran with it.

As far as the forum being "soft"—anybody who would tell us that this was not "hard journalism," I absolutely disagree. The questions were not preselected by the Clinton people. He didn't know if the next question was going to be about the environment or about education or about gun control. He had no idea. That mode of campaigning—we learned in that show, and then later in that forum that was used in the debate—Clinton really knows how to use it. He thinks fast on his feet; he's got so much information in his head.

At least in the particular forum, whether it was a conscious decision on his part going into it that he is not going to be adversarial with anybody, or that's just his "mode," that's just the way he is. With everything that you hear about Clinton and knowing the psychological profile of someone from an alcoholic, broken family who wants to smooth things over and make things better—that's the way he was.

When someone confronted him or had a different opinion, he didn't look at them as "How dare you!" or "You don't know what you're talking about." He looked at them with,

"OK. That's a different opinion." It was more of a respect. These were people who Bill Clinton would work for, the American voters, the American public. The audience of the forum was a slice of that public, the young people who had never been spoken to so directly by a candidate.

NOTES

1. Hammer, Joshua, and Wolfberg, Adam, "Not Just Hit Videos Anymore," *Newsweek*, November 2, 1992, p. 93.

2. De Witt, Karen, "MTV Puts the Campaign on Fast Forward," *The New York Times*, national edition, February 8, 1992, p. B3.

3. Georges, Christopher, "Mock the Vote," *The Washington Monthly*, May, 1993, p. 33.

4. *Ibid.*

6

JEFF GREENFIELD

Jeff Greenfield is a political and media analyst for ABC News and correspondent for ABC News' *Nightline*.

Just before graduating from Yale Law School in 1967, Jeff Greenfield applied for two jobs, a Supreme Court clerkship and a spot in a fellowship program which placed law-school graduates as aides in congressional offices. "Had I gotten the Supreme Court clerkship," says Greenfield, "I would have taken that, but luckily I didn't."

The fellowship program placed him in Senator Robert Kennedy's office. Greenfield was twenty-four years old when he went to Washington that summer. Two days after he arrived, Kennedy needed a speech on the Vietnam War to give in the Senate. That day all the speech writers were gone. "Do you think you could write this?" Kennedy asked Greenfield.

Greenfield consulted aides Arthur Schlesinger and Dick Goodwin and then wrote the speech, the first of many he would write for Kennedy. "Speech writing is a quirky kind of writing," recalls Greenfield. "You either can do it or you can't." Months later when Kennedy's 1968 presidential campaign began, Greenfield went on the road with Kennedy and his chief speech writer, Adam Walinsky. Greenfield still thinks of his time with the campaign as one of the most important experiences of his career. Asked whether Americans tend to view RFK's idealism through rose-tinted glasses, Greenfield is reserved, but blunt: "The best answer is for people to go back and read the speeches and proposals that Kennedy was making. I think they were way ahead of their time . . . and offered a lot of hard-headed, practical possibilities."

After Kennedy's assassination, Greenfield went to work for New York Mayor John V. Lindsay as his chief speech writer. Then in 1970 he began freelancing for David Garth's political consulting firm, Garth Associates, and began writing about new developments in politics and the media. His first book, *The Advance Man*, was published in 1971. Six years later he decided to cross over to journalism completely and started doing television commentary on programs like William Buckley's *Firing Line*. In 1979 Greenfield became a media critic for CBS News, for which he covered the 1980 presidential campaign.

Greenfield joined ABC News in 1983 as a correspondent and political and media analyst; in addition he occasionally anchored ABC News' *Nightline*. In 1988 he debuted as a convention-floor reporter and anchored a series of *Nightline* specials on the '88 campaign. Greenfield also writes a syndicated column and is working on a novel. Among the many books he's authored are *Television: The First 50 Years*, *The Populist Manifesto*, *Playing to Win*, and the *The Real Campaign*.

Greenfield has distinguished himself for bringing more than the usual fare of historical background to his reporting and for not being timid about straying from conventional wisdom. In his book on the 1980 election, *The Real Campaign*, Greenfield countered the widely-held belief that Reagan's triumph was in large part due to the success of the Reagan campaign's image management tactics, arguing that Reagan was an ideological candidate, not an empty-headed actor.[1] Even Reagan's harshest critics now admit that Reagan's political clout primarily derived from an ideological mandate, not his skills as the Great Communicator.

Twenty-five years of experience, as speech writer and political consultant, media critic, and practitioner of journalism, have continually sharpened Greenfield's view of the influence of the press and political handlers. Covering the Clinton administration's travails during it's first months in 1993 for *Nightline*, Greenfield noted, with a taut reserve that belies his analytical zeal, "Odd as it may seem, political operatives and journalists, two professions usually thought of as hopelessly cynical, seem to be telling us the same thing: image and perception only go so far."[2]

There was a lot of pressure to reform campaign coverage after 1988. What was done at ABC News in the way of reform?

What happened in 1988 was all the networks looked up and said, "We can't do this anymore." And I know that there was a very conscious decision here. We said, "We cannot cover campaigns the way we have been covering campaigns. We're prisoners of the campaign trail; we're prisoners of the thought of the day, of the canned comment—we've got to figure out a different way to cover campaigns." And all of the networks in 1992 did very different kinds of work, quite deliberately.

Paul Friedman, who is now executive vice president of ABC News, and Peter Jennings, and Roone Arledge, and Jeff Groulnick, planned a very deliberate way to go outside the mold—to assign beat reporters on things like health and the economy and housing and education, to look at the candidates' proposals and see whether or not they made sense. All the networks subjected the ads and debate claims and speech claims of the candidates to very rigorous—or attempted—very rigorous analysis to see how accurate or inaccurate they were.

What were the things you didn't like about the coverage before?

We'd been treating the campaign trail and the daily appearances of the candidates as the key news of the day and simply saying, "This is what candidate X said, and here's a sound bite," and "Here's what candidate Y said and here's a sound bite." Instead everybody decided to go outside of this mold, to go into communities where the candidates had been or were coming to, and talk to people about what they thought of the campaign relative to their own needs and worries and concerns. Try to take a step out of the campaign rhetoric and say, "What's the record of these candidates? What did Bill Clinton do in Arkansas? How did George Bush govern in four years?"

They would not let the candidates define and limit the parameters of what the coverage was. And if the candidates didn't want to talk about education, that didn't mean that a reporter couldn't go out and look at the record of the candidates and say something intelligent. When Ross Perot emerged, ABC did a one-hour special in which we took a look at different parts of Perot's career, his work at GM, his work on educational reform in Texas, a controversy about a particular development down in Dallas, and the POW issue. And then Perot came on after the local news and did a ninety-minute town meeting with Jennings and an audience.

Nightline *did a report on the media coverage of the Gennifer Flowers story in '92, just after the story broke. The report was criticized as an example of the elite media picking up a sleazy story under the guise of "looking at the media coverage." What do you say to that criticism?*

That story is so widely misunderstood. We had endless debate that day as to whether to do that story, and we ultimately decided to do it because Bill Clinton and Hillary Clinton had tentatively agreed to come on *Nightline* that night and talk about it. That's why we did that story. Then they changed their mind at the last minute, either because of logistics or because they decided to do the *60 Minutes* interview.

We were left at nine o'clock at night with that story, whereupon Clinton's aide, Mandy Grunwald, being a very smart woman, beat the living daylights out of Koppel for doing the story. She basically excoriated us for "slipping into the gutter." But she made a quite powerful point that "why aren't we talking about health care, the economy, crime, foreign policy? Why are we wallowing in this?" And for one of the few times that I can ever remember, in the years I was on *Nightline*, Koppel was clearly on the defensive about this. . . . And that was, from a political point of view, very effective.

We had a story that we were going to do about the primary and the politics, and just very glancingly allude to Gennifer Flowers. Then we were told into the evening that Bill and Hillary wanted to come on and talk about this. So we geared up full speed to do that, and then they decided that they would rather do the *60 Minutes* interview, or maybe the weather was just too bad to get Clinton out or whatever . . . and there we were.

When you originally debated whether to devote the broadcast to the Flowers story, what were your major concerns?

The same concerns that Mandy Grunwald was raising. Is this what a mainstream journalistic organization should be doing at a critical point in a presidential campaign? Do we know whether Gennifer Flowers was telling the truth? Are we dragging this campaign into the gutter? All those were real concerns. But once the Clintons said, "Well, we'd like to come on and confront this," the issue's over. You don't debate that. You don't say to Bill and Hillary Clinton, "We really don't want you to come on *Nightline* and talk about this because it's unseemly." That's asking a little much of any newscast.

What do you think of the view that talk shows have a negative influence on campaigns, because they don't offer the scrutiny of candidates that traditional journalism does?

I think this is an excessive concern. My feeling is that as long as the old-fashioned journalists are free to cover candidates, to point out their weaknesses, to expose their deceits, we're OK. Sure, if you buy an ad or make a speech or go on a talk show where the host is less inquisitive, that's one way to get your message across, but nothing stops reporters, columnists, analysts from going on very well-watched programs and saying, "Here's how this guy's lying" or "Here's how this guy's distorting the truth."

People do look at Perot's success in 1992 and think, "How could someone like Perot succeed without talk shows?"

I think Perot's success in 1992 was a measure of the really profound dissatisfaction with the political system. Now look, forget talk shows, the guy spent sixty-million bucks on paid media mostly. I mean, that obviously had something to do with it. But somebody else could spend sixty million bucks and flop.

It wasn't just that Perot had money, although that was very important. It was that he seemed to be the exact response to the kind of politics people are fed up by—the evasive language, the compromises, the "business as usual." The reason why I think he did as well as he did was people just felt that in some sense some "radical bit of surgery was needed." It's not just that you have access to the public; it's what you are saying, and how does that fit the public sense of what's going on.

How important do you think media relations are to a candidate's success?

I think the whole notion that what happens in the media is determinative of what happens in campaigns is to me a very suspect notion. I mean, you give George Bush a growth rate in 1992 of 3½ percent and you know, MTV and Larry King may matter a lot less. All of the stuff is important on the margins—it's not who wins and who loses. To me where campaigns are won or lost have a lot more to do with what's really out there in the world than how people campaign on the media.

In the book that I did on the 1980 campaign, *The Real Campaign*, what I had to say about that campaign has become conventional wisdom: that what Reagan had is what few presidents or American politicians have, a relatively coherent ideology. He ran on it and he'd spoken for it for twenty years before he got elected president. There's no clearer case of a guy who got elected with an ideological mandate in our recent history than Reagan.

The big shock in Washington was when Reagan got elected he proceeded to do precisely what he said he was going to do—huge defense buildup, big tax cut, try to get regulators off business's back. And whether that was the right or wrong policy, Reagan did what he said he was going to do. The argument of my book was that the press in covering all this stuff, in looking at the media, missed the fact that this was a very significant political decision by the country to change course dramatically. And the person who they were following was a guy who was one of the most clear-cut ideological candidates we have ever produced.

Now it was also true that he was weak on a lot of facts, that he was careless about what was real and what was fantasy. But this was an amazing campaign, very unusual for the American politics, where a very clearly defined ideological candidate with a very clear set of policies was what people were responding to. They had made a political judgment that not only the incumbent administration, but the whole direction of the country was politically wrong. And they wanted it to change dramatically and Reagan offered them that. That to me was what 1980 was about. Not whether or not Reagan looked good on television.

So you don't believe that Reagan's style of media management played a major role in his success?

I recounted all kinds of terrible Reagan mistakes on the air. They were reported, they were laughed at, they were featured in network newscasts. All kinds of media gaffes that we would consider devastating. And the reason why it didn't hurt Reagan was because people felt they knew who this guy was in a political sense. I think what they got, which I would regard as fundamentally accurate, was that this guy had a very firm—or if you didn't like him "rigid"—set of beliefs.

I think we've grown up in a time when both the press and the politicians believe that the media are the determinative factor. And my argument has always been that, well, it counts; you've got to pay attention to it, but it counts on the margins. It can do some things. It can get you well known; it'll help if you know how to use the media to convey a certain image, like Clinton's bus tour in the 1992 campaign.

But we're overrating it in terms of the campaign as well as in terms of governing. By and large, George Bush lost in 1992 because the economy was in really bad shape, because the Republicans lost three of the most important arguments they had been making to the voters in the last dozen or more years. They lost "foreign affairs strength," because things went too well and nobody cared. They lost "economic growth," not because of the media, but because the growth stopped. And they lost "taxes," because Bush felt he had to go back on that 1988 promise. Those factors are so much more important than how a candidate does or doesn't do on television, that I think it's silly to talk about this as though media performance is the key to whether you win or lose.

When Bush ran against Dukakis, the Communist threat was still very real; the Reagan record on foreign affairs was pretty damn good overall. Bush had much more experience than Dukakis, an appeal that still mattered to people, and economic growth was chugging along. The fact that Dukakis rode in a tank didn't help him obviously. But look at where the country thought it was in 1988. By and large Reagan had done an effective job. Bush ran as Reagan's heir and Dukakis was seen as this guy that didn't really have a grip on the importance of foreign affairs and was out of touch with the values of a lot of Americans.

One of the things that Clinton did in 1992, and this isn't a media strategy nearly as much as it is a political strategy in the broader sense, is Clinton ran as a "pro death penalty, tough on crime, end welfare as we know it, jobs and growth Democrat." Which hadn't been done for a while. But those are not media matters, those ought to be thought of, in my view, as political matters.

Has there been in your mind a close presidential election in the last thirty years where media relations played an important role?

I think if you look at the 1976 Carter-Ford race, even though neither of them were what you'd call "media stars," it made more of a difference there, because the issues were less dramatic. I think the fact that Carter was positioned as a kind of fairy tale, "man of the people, carries his own garment bag" man made a difference. But again, remember the overhang of 1976, coming out of Watergate. That was a very unusual political climate.

The other argument is that Ford closed as well as he did because his media campaign was very effective. He came from thirty points down and lost by about two. He had very effective advertising. His media campaign raised very effectively some doubts about Carter, that Carter was not a person of principle, that he did not have the breadth of experience necessary to run the country. And they communicated that message well, but it was in a context where there weren't great issues on the table.

When Carter tried to do that to Reagan—Carter ran the same kind of ads that Ford had run against him, describing Reagan as a "simplistic, trigger-happy, dangerous" kind of guy—it didn't work, because people really were sufficiently fed up with Carter to say, "We've got to get somebody else in here." And the Bush campaign tried much the same tactic against Clinton, but the political terrain was different and it didn't stick.

What about the accusation that Carter was really chewed up by the news media and that's one of the main reasons he lost in 1980?

I think that when you have a massive recession that cripples the industrial heartland of America, when you have inflation running at an annualized rate of as much as 20 percent in the spring of 1980, when your foes in the world appear to have taken the offensive, and when half of your own party is trying to dump you in favor of a challenger—I regard those as political rather than media problems, by and large.

The hostage thing is trickier. I would argue media made a difference in the Hostage Crisis. I think the fact that Walter Cronkite signed off every night by counting down the number of days that the hostages were in captivity, that the precursor to *Nightline*, called *America Held Hostage*, certainly elevated the Hostage Crisis to a level that in strict geopolitical terms it probably didn't deserve. But I would also argue that you had the complicity of the Carter administration. For its own political reasons it made the Hostage Crisis front and center. Carter refused to leave the White House, wouldn't light the Christmas tree star until the hostages were released. It was a joint effort to exaggerate the importance of the Hostage Crisis.

I get exasperated by this argument because it tends to put the stage above the play. And I think that's wrong. I heard once one person describe years ago the visit of John Paul II to Poland as a "media event." As though the return of the first Polish-born pope to his homeland would have been a nonevent if television hadn't been there! It's just not, in my view, what's at stake. Nixon, who was one of the least "mediagenic" figures in American history, managed to spend four years in office and get reelected in what I believe the single biggest margin of victory in American political history. What does that tell you?

My argument is not an absolutist argument. For instance, the televised debates in 1960 made a difference. Remember, when you have an election decided by one tenth of 1 percent of the vote you can pretty well argue that anything hit the balance. Maybe it was Robert Kennedy's phone call to the jail where Martin Luther King, Jr., was. But I don't argue that the first time we had television debates in history and that seventy million people are watching and Nixon looks like he's about to die, that it doesn't have an impact. But you also need to remember that in 1968 Richard Nixon went into the general election leading Hubert Humphrey by fifteen points, outspent him two to one, and beat him by one point. Now how successful was that?

I mean, how important is the media compared to the fact that the Democratic party had been ripped to shreds by the argument over Vietnam in 1968 and the perception of a lot of the country was that, between Vietnam and domestic riots, the incumbent president had literally lost control of things? And how important was it that in a lot of key states George Wallace siphoned off millions of traditional Democratic votes? Where do you lay that stuff up, compared to whether or not Nixon had a better message in '68 than '60?

My argument is not that television doesn't matter. I would not advise, if I were still advising politicians, any politician running for president to forget the media. I would only say that the role it plays in elections needs to be put in its proper place. I think what goes into advertising and how a president or a candidate communicates and how they look on television matters, but it matters in context. It's not the be-all and end-all of campaigns. If you had given George Bush 4½ percent growth from January to November of 1992, he would have been almost certainly reelected and all the bus tours and all the "Arsenios" and all the "Larry Kings" and "MTVs" wouldn't have changed that.

NOTES

1. Greenfield, Jeff, *The Real Campaign: How the Media Missed the Story of the 1980 Campaign* (New York: Summit Books, 1982), p. 23.

2. ABC News, *Nightline*, June 29, 1993.

7

GERALDINE FERRARO

Geraldine Ferraro was the first woman nominated by a major party to run for Vice President of the United States.

In July 1984 the Democratic convention in San Francisco overflowed with euphoria. Teary-eyed delegates held up bouquets of flowers and "Fritz and a Ms." signs, chanting, "Geerr-eee, Geerr-eee." A handsome, middle-aged woman with tawny-gray hair beamed at the crowd from the podium. "There are no doors we cannot unlock. . . . If we can do this, we can do anything."

Geraldine Ferraro was making history. In a few quick weeks, she'd gone from a little-known congresswoman to the first woman nominated by a major party to run for vice president. In 1984 Fritz Mondale faced a highly popular Ronald Reagan. Ferraro was a daring choice for a running mate and her candidacy gave the campaign a new, unpredictable sense of momentum. But amid the heady feeling of limitlessness at the convention, no one would have predicted what would happen in the weeks to come.

A month later Ferraro was mired in the "Ferraro-Zaccaro finances," a story that dominated the media and crippled the Democrats' ability to get their message out for weeks. Ferraro and her husband, John Zaccaro, were accused of financial wrongdoing and connections to organ-

ized crime. Added to the "integrity gap" stories were questions about Ferraro's character. As a woman, was she prepared to be a heartbeat away from the presidency? Did she know enough about foreign policy? Could she really serve as a commander in chief?

Ferraro fought off many of these doubts successfully. Many speculated she'd buckle under the pressure of the allegations brought against her and be dropped from the ticket. At an August press conference in 1984, in which she sought to put to rest questions about her finances, Ferraro surprised many with her steadiness and grit as she fielded questions before a hotel ballroom crammed with reporters and TV cameras. Unfortunately for Ferraro, the campaign was only the beginning of the stories about her family's finances.

Nearly a decade later the accusations still plague her. For years after the '84 campaign, Ferraro and her husband waded through an onslaught of investigations. Some evidence of wrongdoing was uncovered—her husband did plead guilty to a misdemeanor in connection with a real-estate deal.[1] Added to this, Ferraro's son was convicted for selling cocaine to an undercover agent while at college in Middlebury, Vermont. Ferraro protested each accusation at every step, sometimes convincingly, often in the glaring spotlight of the media.

In the late eighties there was a reprieve. The investigations seemed to be put to rest, and it looked as if Ferraro might be able to resuscitate her public image. She launched a campaign for the Democratic Senate nomination in New York and campaigned tirelessly all over the state, but lost in a brutal primary runoff in 1992 in which old questions about her husband's business dealings and purported Mafia ties destroyed her candidacy. The primary's gruesome mudslinging left New York voters queasy and seemed to finish Ferraro's political career for good.

To investigate conclusively all the accusations against
Ferraro would be an almost endless task. Just try to get
to the bottom of any one of these stories and you're neck-
deep in FEC filings, FBI reports, court transcripts. Most
of the investigations would never have occurred except for
Ferraro's celebrity. In an *L.A. Times* editorial, a Washing-
ton-based lawyer, Constance O'Keefe, wrote that Ferraro
was yet another example that "the human cost of running
for public office has become much too high."[2] But mean-
while, the accusations, lacking any clear truth or falsity,
continued to mar Ferraro's public image.

So, for many of us, Ferraro is a troubling figure, appealing, yet hard to trust. Left to our instincts and media
savvy, our compass needles are still dizzy, still trying to
find north. In person Ferraro is convincing and genuine—
direct, funny, unpretentious. Most of us feel that something terribly unfair happened to her in '84. "If I wanted
this kind of abuse," snaps the television character Murphy Brown, "I'd run for vice president." Most Americans
want to believe Ferraro, a woman who stood for so much,
for a new role for women in American politics. But even
many devoted fans of Ferraro have begun to have misgiv-
ings.

Whether another chapter in her political life will be
written remains to be seen. Looking back at the 1984
presidential campaign, most Democratic insiders agree
with Ferraro that Republican operatives floated the original rumors that triggered the stories about her finances.
And that the "Ferraro-Zaccaro finances" was such a juicy
investigative story that the media blew it way out of
proportion. But few would contend that Mondale lost to
the extraordinarily popular Ronald Reagan because of
what happened to Ferraro. What Ferraro's troubles did do
was stall out the Democratic campaign, dimming the

unpredictable glow of her candidacy, which at first looked as if it could give the Democratic ticket a winning edge.

Broadcast journalists are criticized for focusing too much on "character issues" in presidential campaigns. Do you think television news focuses too much on character?

Well, part of the problem is in defining character. Do I think that it's important that someone have great moral character? I think it's important that people have a certain morality, but I'm not quite sure if I judge their moral character on whether or not they've had any premarital or extramarital affairs; I just don't. It's not my choice of things to do, and certainly if it were my husband I'd be outraged. But I don't know if I'd be outraged as much by the fact that it's immoral as I would be because I felt I had been wronged, I mean; it's that type of thing. You take your wedding vows and you stick to them, that's what they're about.

When I'm looking at a public official, what I'm much more concerned about is not, for instance, whether or not he sees his grandchildren on Sunday—which, you know, Ronald Reagan didn't see his grandchildren until they were, what, a year and half? There are certain people who would think that was immoral.

But what I'm interested in is how they feel on moral issues like feeding people who cannot afford to feed themselves. What is our obligation as a people toward other human beings? Those are the moral questions that I have to debate and I have to feel comfortable with a candidate. I have to feel comfortable on issues of nuclear war and disarmament. Those are moral issues. So, is a person's moral character of importance? Yes, but I must say that I judge people's morality in a different way from what is happening now.

The entire world would love to see a "perfect" person run this country. It is not going to happen. And you can have people who are caring, loving husbands, fathers, grandfathers; maybe they've never cheated on their income tax, never plagiarized anything, but they could be terrible leaders for this nation. That's not what I want to judge people on. I want to judge people on their ideas and on their stance on issues and what they've done in the past that will reflect what they're going to do in the future as concerns the important things that face this nation.

What about the view that it's important to know if a candidate cheats in his private life, because if he cheats, for instance, on his wife, who knows what he may do in government?

I think it's silly. Reporters will attempt to justify what I consider an invasion of privacy by saying, "Well, if he did it there, he'll do it someplace else." That's not sufficient justification. There is a difference between a person's private life and their public actions.

Richard Nixon's private life was above reproach. One would therefore assume, taking the journalist's argument to a full extreme, that he should have been the most moral of individuals, the man with the greatest amount of integrity, because according to all the records, he never cheated on his wife. One does not follow the other. What a candidate does with his wife or doesn't do with his wife or whether or not he's gay or not gay—I'm not going to make a moral judgment on that according to my moral standards. It's not my business. I don't have to know that in order to determine whether or not he understands the economy, whether or not he has compassion for somebody else. I think the press will try to justify looking into that in order to cover it, and use the First Amendment allowance they have. And I think it's fictitious.

What about the story of your finances in '84?

Well, it's legitimate to find out what people have their money into; that's important to know, because it might show a conflict—that people are working for their own benefit in government. If you are working in government, you're really supposed to be working for the good of the country. People had a right to know that, and so they had a right to know whether or not I filed my taxes, paid my taxes, whether or not I did something in my time in Congress to benefit my husband's business. That's totally legitimate.

My problem with the press was that they wanted to know immediately. My second problem was that I had a big mouth and said, "I'm not going to release my husband's returns." It would have been a lot easier if I had just released them, but I didn't. And I didn't know how to operate with the press, and it was partly my fault.

I had to answer every question in order to assure them that I wasn't hiding anything. We got the accountants to put it all together—accountants who would certify that whatever we were saying was absolutely true. And we had thirty days to do it. So we took the full thirty days. When we finally had done it, we figured if we distributed this stuff our press offices would get hundreds of calls—"Would you explain this? Would you explain that?" So we decided, and it was my suggestion, to do a press conference. I wanted to do a press conference and answer the questions once and for all.

Now I must tell you, I cheated a bit, in that I am very comfortable in interviews. I don't have problems, I don't have anything to hide, so I am honest and it usually comes through. The side benefit was that people kept on saying, "How can she do under strain? Can she take tension [laughing]? She's in her late forties. . . . Is she menopausal?" Everybody was concerned. And they didn't know whether I'd be able to deal with pressure without tears. And so we positively said, "Let's go ahead with a press conference."

In that conference we showed that I could operate under real tight pressure. The press conference lasted almost two hours. There were 200 people there—they went on and on. But what happened was it became obvious that I wasn't going to be intimidated by the press; I wasn't going to be rattled by them. I could handle it—certainly nobody was under any greater tension than I was.

George Bush, and I do like George Bush, I mean [smiling], not as my candidate, not as my president—he was unable to handle the press. He'd come off a plane and shout. And you've seen President Reagan; he was a disaster in his press conferences. He was really prepped—they spent days getting him ready and he was still a disaster. I think if you were to set Reagan down and ask him any details about Iran-contra, he couldn't handle it.

I was told that in 1988 George Bush was told that he should do a "Ferraro." This was on the Iran-contra arms sale. It'd been suggested that he do a press conference, let the press ask as many questions as they want, and answer them all. Whether or not he'll do that I don't know, but I find it interesting that I am now becoming a noun.

Was it just bad luck that the media attention to your finances came all at once in the month after the Democratic convention in 1984?

No, it was a deliberate action by the Republicans. The week after I got the nomination the Washington Legal Foundation and the Fund for a Conservative Majority, both connected to the White House, had filed complaints against me at the Justice Department based on my 1978 FEC filings. The FEC had cleared me in 1978 and the Ethics Committee cleared me in December of '84 of wrongdoing, but the Justice Department was the Meese Justice Department, and it was used politically.

And what they did was they conducted an investigation—actually hundreds of thousands of dollars of the American taxpayer's money spent with the FBI trying to find out whether or not we were connected to organized crime. It was absolutely appalling. And it was common knowledge that I was going to run for the Senate in '86, so it was dragged out for a quite a long period of time after the presidential campaign.

This is a rather strange story, but in 1985 an FBI agent called my husband's office in New York and asked to meet with him. He was told that my husband had gone down to Washington to see his lawyer, Steve Pollack. The FBI agent asked if he could come see him that day at the lawyer's office in Washington. And when they met, the FBI agent said to my husband, "We have just gotten information that there is a contract on your life and that you're going to be killed." My husband and Pollack looked at him in absolute disbelief. My husband's reaction was—"Who?" and "When?" The FBI agent said, "Well, we don't know who, but it's going to happen today in Washington sometime."

So, the lawyer almost had a heart attack and my husband looked at him and said, "You've got to be kidding!" The FBI guy says, "Can I ask you some questions? Do you know someone by the name of Genovese?" My husband said, "Sure, there's a Genovese drugs store, and there's a guy by the name of Tony Genovese, who's a lawyer. . . ." The FBI agent said, "No, no, no . . . that's not who I'm talking about. I'm talking about Genovese, the crime family."

The FBI agent went on, "These are two people down in Florida. Do you know them?" And my husband said, "The only people I know in Florida are my uncle and aunt, who retired down in Florida. . . ." John then turned around to the agent and said, "When are you guys going to believe that I don't know anybody involved in organized crime?" At which point my husband said to the lawyer, "This is all a bunch of garbage. I'm leaving." When I saw John later that day and heard the story, we both started to laugh because we, more than anybody in the world, we know that organized crime is not the least bit interested in us, because we don't know anything about them and we're not involved with them.

That was in September of 1985. We have never seen or heard anything more about it and though I got my FBI report under the Freedom of Information Act, there is absolutely no reference to either the phone conversation, to the visit of the FBI in the Washington office, or to anything at all that would indicate that there is any semblance of truth to the entire story. Probably the only people who would admit that meeting took place are me, my husband, and Steve Pollack, the lawyer who was sitting in the office that day. That was the type of thing that was done throughout the campaign and throughout the investigation by the Meese people.

You know, it makes me sound almost paranoid, but I'm not. There are so many connections, so many times that I would have friends of mine repeat conversations that they had overheard. But there's no doubt that the FBI was being used by Meese for political purposes. When these people do these things, they don't say—a candidate never attacks directly, it's always rumors and planting of whispers—I mean, it's horrendous stuff.

When I got the nomination at the Democratic Convention in '84 the polls were dead even. The Republicans, I've been told, looked at the polls and said, "Oh my God! How do we deal with it?" And the way you deal with it is—if I could make a difference, then you go after me and you destroy me. So the Republicans were the ones who initiated it. But the press had its piece in it. What the Republicans would do is go to friendly people in the press—even unfriendly, objective reporters—and say, "Well, you know, these are things that are there; perhaps you might be interested in some information that we have." That's not unusual. That's done all the time, people dropping off little hints and leaks to reporters for them to follow up.

What would you say to voters who—even if they have not been convinced by the allegations—have doubts about you?

You have to look at the source of the accusation. I look at it as being anti-Italian and I'm one of the people who's becoming a leading force speaking out against this kind of thing. I've been speaking out when people have done it to blacks, and to Jews, and to gays. People just don't seem to think it's important when it happens with Italians. But I speak up about that too.

None of the people whom I know believe it. The unfortunate thing that happened in this last race was that it was enough to raise doubts. . . . It is impossible to disprove a negative. And we could not prove that we had no connections. Of course, nobody could prove that we did have some. All you had was innuendo. Society has got to deal with these stereotypes.

Putting that aside, what do you think the media most missed about you during the '84 presidential campaign that was important?

What they really missed was that I knew the issues, that I was able to handle them. And what they missed as a whole was that Fritz Mondale was telling the truth about the campaign. And we can sit back now and say, "Ha, I told you so!"

My daughter worked for Solomon Brothers, and they invited me to come down and speak to some of the vice presidents. I went down during the 1984 campaign and I

will never forget it. I was talking about the budget deficit
and there were a lot of people sitting there when we talked
about deficits that kind of sluffed them off, "Well, the
economy's growing. . . ." And three years later you have
Black Monday, and the first thing Wall Street does is turn
around and say, "Washington! Why don't you do something
about those deficits?" I mean, where the hell were you? We
were telling you about that three years ago; it's not something brand new!

But nobody wanted to hear that then. And so what you
do is you turn around and you say, what happened in 1984
was that people weren't listening; they got caught up in
"my husband," they got caught up in my wardrobe, silli-
ness . . . I mean, "Is she strong enough?" Is she strong
enough to do what? She's not "strong enough" to push a
button—she's strong enough to get peace for this country
and for this world. Those are things that are important.
Certainly nobody asked that question about Maggie
Thatcher.

*Ted Koppel was accused of questioning you differently
because you were a female candidate and that it was unfair.
But Koppel is tough on everybody. He was very tough on
Dukakis in '88. What was the difference?*

Well, Ted Koppel was very heavy on Dukakis. He came at
him very strong, as I recall the interview, but it was not
the same type of thing. Here he was questioning my
knowledge. He was debating semantics, virtually questioning whether or not I knew the difference between
"adding" or "building"—whether I knew what was going
on, whether we were getting rid of weapons and substitut-
ing them. That would not have been done with anybody
else.

He wouldn't have done it with Lloyd Bentsen. I don't
think he would have done it with Dukakis either, that type
of thing. I have to tell you, the reaction when I walked out

of the Koppel show was amazing—Lynn Sherr was outside, from ABC News, along with other women reporters—
they were furious. The reporters were absolutely livid.

*In other words, Koppel wasn't asking you about issues
and how you would handle them; he was asking, "Do you
understand weapon systems?"*

Yeah—"Explain why you think that . . ." and "Are you
absolutely sure that what you've said is right?" I had done
Meet the Press with Marvin Kalb and Marvin asked me,
would I be "strong enough to push the button?" And I said,
you know, I hoped I'd be strong enough to be able to go
through the whole process of reducing tensions so that
there would be no need to "push the button." When I spoke
to him afterwards I said, "Why did you ask me that
question? Would you ask that of a man?" And he said, "Well
I have on two occasions." And the two occasions were both
religious people. I was not a minister. I had none of the
restrictions that a minister might have. So therefore I
should have been treated like any other senator, member
of Congress. I mean, Gerry Ford, I'm sure Kalb didn't ask,
"Would you be strong enough to push the button?" And
that's the difference—I was treated as if genetically I
couldn't understand the differences in weapons.

With Marvin Kalb the question was, am I "genetically
tough enough to handle . . . ?" The thing about it is, that
you sit back and you watch what happens over a period of
time. . . . When I saw Bud McFarland—after his involvement in the Iran-contra scandal, after I saw him react as
he did to his arrest and respond by attempting to commit
suicide. I was amazed. If that man were running for vice
president of the United States, Ted Koppel would never
have challenged him. And Marvin Kalb would never have
said to him, "Are you strong enough to push the button?"

Now, Gerry Ferraro doesn't attempt suicide when she
runs into problems, and neither does her kid. So you look

and you say, "These guys, because they're men, because they're former Marines, they're tough . . ."—automatically the presumption is there, of competence and of toughness. With me, the burden shifted. The presumption was of weakness—I had to prove myself to Ted Koppel! And I have to tell something; he knew he was doing it, because he apologized. . . . It's television. Ted Koppel is a personality as well as a reporter. He's a good interviewer, no doubt about it; I enjoy watching him most of the time. But he's a personality, just like Sam Donaldson is a personality.

"How smart Ted Koppel is" was another part of the program. He was doing all this stuff on my knowledge of strategic weapons . . . garbage . . . and he admits that the interview was terrible. I responded to the questions, but when I finished the interview, there were women crazed about his arrogance. Part of it was Ted Koppel was selling Ted Koppel.

He's trying to get better ratings?

I wouldn't say he's doing that totally, but I kind of think that has to be a piece of it, and that's not a negative. I mean no more than doing something to sell your newspapers isn't totally negative. As long as it's balanced there's nothing wrong with it. When I was a trial attorney, when I went into court, I played to the jury; I wanted to win. I wanted to get a conviction; I believed that the person I was prosecuting was guilty.

To say that he's doing it only for the ratings, well, I don't think that's fair either. I do think that he's a very legitimate reporter, but part of it is theater; it has to be. We all make our living doing a little bit of theater. Politicians do, too.

What do you think of the view that talk shows are a dangerous replacement for conventional journalism be-

cause there are, for instance, less stringent ethical guide-lines for stories, fewer follow-up questions?

I think you're seeing a bunch of Washington reporters who say they don't like the competition. I think this is fine. The press likes to filter the information. You can do an interview and when you get finished with the interview what is in that interview is what that reporter wants to write. What's in the television interview is what the reporter and producer want to put on and it's limited by the amount of time.

Bill Clinton went out and went over their heads. He went directly to the people. He used Phil Donahue's show to talk to the people, to take questions from the people. He used Larry King for the same purpose. Ross Perot also did it. I think it's terrific. I've always done well in that medium, because you get through—you stop having the media filter the information that gets to the people. You go directly to the people.

Bush had become very isolated after twelve years in the White House. I mean, who do you talk to? You talk to each other and you talk to the press. And you don't get out . . . unless Clinton continues to do it, unless he reaches over his staff and reaches over the media to go back to the people, which is what he did in the 1992 campaign, I'm afraid he might become insulated too. It's part of the nature of that office.

NOTES

1. O'Keefe, Constance, "The Famous Get Justice with a Vengeance," *Los Angeles Times*, October 23, 1987, section II, p. 9.
2. *Ibid.*

8

BERNARD SHAW

Bernard Shaw is the Cable News Network's Principal
Washington Anchor.

Etched in the history of presidential debates is Bernard
Shaw's question to Michael Dukakis in 1988—"Governor,
if Kitty Dukakis were raped and murdered, would you
favor an irrevocable death penalty for the killer?" As soon
as Shaw finished his question, Dukakis launched into an
emotionless exposition of his views on capital punishment,
confirming many voters' fears that he was a liberal ide-
ologue without the character or passion needed to fill the
shoes of the president. It was a harsh example of what
happens when a candidate fails to conjure up emotion at
a critical moment.

After the debate, Democrats were despondent and Republicans were in a state of glee. The Dukakis campaign,
already a sinking dirigible, now had a huge gash in its side.
An army of pundits descended on Dukakis's wooden response. Shaw's question was described by some as a "fat
pitch disguised as a bean ball"[1]—Dukakis should have
milked it for all the emotion it was worth. Others saw it
as the "killer question" that brought Dukakis down—for
Democrats, a cruel stumbling block; for Republicans, a
revealing probe into Dukakis's brittle temperament. But

for Bernard Shaw, it was simply doing his job—asking tough, relevant questions—something which he's approached with a distinctive deliberateness for over thirty years.

Shaw signed on with CNN as its principal anchor just as it began its operations in 1980. As CNN grew to be one of the globe's most influential news outlets, Shaw became internationally known as America's "fourth anchor." Shaw was ready to make the leap to anchordom when he joined CNN. He had served as a Washington correspondent for CBS News from 1971 to 1977, and then as a correspondent and bureau chief for ABC News. Before joining CBS, he was a reporter for Westinghouse Broadcasting Company's Group W.

CNN was a risky venture when Shaw signed on. Entrepreneur Ted Turner's twenty-four-hour news network was originally the laughingstock of many news-business insiders. But in a few short years the "Chicken Noodle Network" would snap the three major networks' monopoly on news reporting and by the end of the decade become the largest news-gathering organization in the world. CNN now reaches over 50 million cable households in the United States, and is one of the chief conduits for the "global electronic village," reaching 30 million households in over one hundred countries. Walk into any television newsroom in the United States or abroad and you're likely to find a monitor tuned to CNN.

CNN's first significant bite out of the three networks' turf came in 1982, when it won a lawsuit against ABC, CBS, NBC, and the White House to gain equal participation in the White House press pool. Its live broadcasts of critical events such as the *Challenger* disaster, the Iran-contra hearings, and the fall of the Berlin Wall forced the networks to retool their coverage. Because of CNN, news is now almost always instantaneous, so the networks have to be much more than simply "gatekeepers" of breaking news.

CNN's Gulf War coverage was what sealed its fate as one of the premier news reporting outlets. Shaw had gone to Baghdad for an interview with Saddam Hussein in 1991 when the allied bombing of Iraq commenced. From the ninth floor of a hotel, with bombs dropping just blocks away, Shaw and CNN reporters Peter Arnett and John Holliman were the only journalists to report on the invasion live from Bagdhad. CNN's continous coverage of the first night of the Allied Forces' bombing was watched around the globe by over a billion viewers.

Since its beginnings, Shaw has overseen CNN's presidential campaign coverage, anchoring most of the network's special coverage of presidential campaigns, including coverage of the primaries, conventions, and election night. In addition, he has anchored CNN's series of *Inside Politics* specials on presidential campaigns.

What do you say to the view that the pressure on network news divisions to make money, which increased around 1980, has made news reporting less substantive and more vulnerable to manipulation by media handlers?

I think that's a long leap into speculation. I really do. I and my network were part of the economic earthquake in broadcast journalism. CNN changed the economics of television news for all time to come in my judgment. Basically because we did, and do, more with less money. Ours is a very tightly run network. We squeeze a Lincoln off a five-dollar bill.

One of the reasons is that for all practical purposes we're a nonunion network. Some of our camera crews are union, but in the main we are much leaner, and we've been able to devote a lot of our resources to covering the news. And that's one of the prime reasons for the networks' cutting back in staffing stories and personnel.

And on the side of the entertainment networks, NBC, ABC, and CBS, there was a quantum change in the attitude of the owners of networks. Just as CNN was coming into stride, the owners of networks stopped tolerating red ink from their news divisions. Before a news division was considered the "crown jewel" of prestige in a network's operation, and losses were tolerated. Because of what CNN was doing, and because networks had become owned by companies that were strictly bottom line in their orientation, they started insisting that their news divisions be profit centers. So a shakeout began.

But I don't agree that networks, because of their economic problems, consciously or unconsciously, facilitated the Reagan administration's propaganda and PR efforts. I reject that out of hand, that contention. Ronald Reagan's existence and the problems of the networks did not dilute the journalism that correspondents had been practicing before this became a crisis.

Critics cite incidents from the Reagan era as examples of the press playing into efforts at manipulation—for example, the scenes with Reagan on a helicopter pad with the press yelling questions at him. Reagan appears on the news as "that sweet old man, he wants to talk to the press, but he can't hear them. . ." and there are those nasty journalists yelling at him. Critics ask, Why did the press play into that and continue to yell at Reagan and why did they air clips of these scenes? What do you say to such criticism?

If you forget that the White House and the White House staff collectively are a tightly organized group committed to the image of the president, the boss of that staff—if you forget that, then you will not understand the negatives under which a reporter works at the White House. Our critics who cite that and our shouting over rotor blades to try to get a question to the president of the United States, forget that whenever the White House and the president want to say something and want it heard, miraculously, the rotor blades are off. The White House controls that, and that's very important to remember. And if a president is so inaccessible that reporters are reduced to shouting questions at him over rotor blades, then so be it. We have to try to do our jobs.

And you recall there were a lot of rotor blades, a lot of helicopters going during the Iran-contra scandal, for example. A president is always most accessible when that president is riding high in the polls and when he and his staff believe it's positive for him to be in public. The moment something goes wrong, the moment there's a crisis, or mistakes are made, a president suddenly is not available to the news media.

So you cover the inaccessibility?

You cover the president of the United States as best you can. If the White House staff does not want you to have access to the president to ask questions about sensitive matters, you're not going to have access to the president, period.

Going into the 1992 campaign, what were the most important things you kept in mind in terms of shaping the overall coverage?

I resolved, as did most journalists in print or broadcast, to insist on tracking issues much better and to constantly come back to them. And not to make the mistake in previous campaigns of tiring of reporting on the issues merely because we had, as is natural in the early primary season, virtually covered them to death.

The mistake that journalists have made in the past is to undercover the issues during the middle part of the campaign, mainly during the summer convention season, and not to return to the issues until the closing weeks before Election Day in November. That was one promise I strove to keep.

Another one was to concentrate faithfully on the money. Money is the juice of politics. And the third was to be extremely vigilant and watchful for nuance and slight change in the candidates' rhetoric, in their positions on issues, and for changes in their campaign styles, the tone of their speeches, the tone of their ads.

And I would add a fourth: that is, to really police the ads. The phenomenon of the attack ad—and a lot of political analysts agree—really undercuts a lucid, thoughtful discussion and airing of issues. And we really watched ads and reported on ads very religiously almost.

In working harder to cover issues in the middle of the campaign in 1992, what did you do, more specifically?

Revisiting and restating the issues—doing that enabled us to not become preoccupied with the horse race. Of course polls were part of the reportage, everyone was polling. But to remind—not the voters, because the voters know damn well the issues they care about—but to *remind the candidates* that the voters care about issues. And actually our job was enhanced by the preoccupation, the near total preoccupation with the economy, the economy, the economy and, of course, jobs.

And in terms of watching for nuances and changes in a candidate's rhetoric, could you give an example?

One example was the very definable and clear decision by the Clinton camp to respond blow for blow to any charge made against the candidate during the campaign. And this had its genesis in the reporting on the Gennifer Flowers allegations, I believe.

In 1988 Bob Dole committed a horrific mistake in the New Hampshire primary. When coming out of the Iowa caucuses he was feeling very good about how he did and he allowed George Bush to run an attack ad whose charges went unchallenged for two days, and it cost Dole the New Hampshire primary. Apparently, Bill Clinton learned a lot from that episode, and you recall how he answered, virtually hourly if not daily, any charge, any allegation. That was a very important development, a very important nuance to report and to track because it showed a lot about Clinton's attitude and character as a fighter.

And of course recent history bore out that it was smart to follow that. He never gave up; he never stopped when he was down, when he didn't have a major win until Super Tuesday, when he finally won in his home region, the South. And we've seen that time and again from the time when his economic stimulus package was throttled by the Republicans to this most recent win, of his budget plan, his deficit-reduction plan, in the uphill fight.

It was the first opportunity for voters to get a window on the makeup of this man, his moxie, his chutzpah. It was an inkling of it—the coverage of how he responded to attacks, how he responded to the Gennifer Flowers episode, and other things in the campaign.

A lot of voters feel that they are able to get more perspective on a candidate's character through talk shows. Do you think the increased number of appearances by candidates on talk shows helps or hurts the selection process?

I applaud it. I stand applauding the efforts by politicians to make, in their minds, "end-runs" around us and so-called "break out of the filter" and take their message directly to the people. I applaud that, because the more politicians expose themselves, regardless of the forum, the more voters are going to understand these politicians and understand the issues. I don't feel slighted one whit.

What do you say to the view that talk shows overemphasize personality and that candidates can distort the truth about their history and the issues much more, because there are no journalists there to follow up on their statements?

Well to some extent that's true, but people who say that forget that viewers are *watching* and listening to claims made by these politicians, and personality *is* an important element in a voter's decision-making process. People forget that American voters feel very visceral about their president or someone who would be president. They have to feel that they *know* this person; they want to try to get to know this person. They want to think that "this president represents me and believes in what I believe in."

So "feel" and "personality" and those other intangible elements are very important. Issues are important too, but the element of the personality is very, very important. That was one of Dukakis's major problems. In all our tracking polls, in exit polls in 1988, people repeatedly said they didn't feel Dukakis; they didn't get a sense of warmth.

I'm just telling you what people were telling us. Bush called Dukakis "the ice man" twice during that campaign. And he did that because of what focus groups had told the Republicans and the Bush people about perceptions of Dukakis. And it certainly was one of the reasons why I phrased the question the way I did in the '88 debate, in the second debate between Dukakis and Bush.

Would you describe how you came up with that question, your thought process?

Well the thought process lasted two agonizing days. I as moderator was restricted in the number of questions I could ask. The moderator could ask only two questions, unlike the panelists, who asked many questions on varying subjects. Therefore my question to each candidate had to be, in my judgment, the *epitome* of the issues in the campaign.

And because I decided that my question had to be that and since I'm a journalist, even though I'm the moderator, I was under great strain to formulate a question that went to the heart of the campaign. I went back over all the issues in the campaign, I went back over the positions taken by the candidates, and repeatedly asked myself, What question can you ask Dukakis?

The elements of that question included the following: Crime, obviously, was a very emotional issue in that campaign. The death penalty was an issue in that campaign; Bush favored it, Dukakis did not. I don't know whether "credibility" is the right word, but the issue of personality and warmth and compassion formed a kind of undercurrent in that campaign: George Bush calling Dukakis "the ice man" twice; Dukakis being accused of being a robot, a computer with no feeling.

These elements were out there, they'd been debated, they'd been discussed. Polling data had indicated that voters did not doubt Dukakis's competency—he was a very competent executive, a governor of a state—but they didn't *feel* anything. So as I thought about these elements, the question I came up with was the question—"Governor, if Kitty Dukakis were raped and murdered, would you favor an irrevocable death penalty for the killer?"

Conversely, with George Bush, one of the prime issues in the campaign became his selection of a vice-presidential running mate, Dan Quayle. I mean, this man became an issue. Who was he? How competent was he? Why would Bush pick such an unknown? And then the reporting started and the news media dug and reported the fact that Dan Quayle had been campaigning for a long time to be selected to the ticket. And voters were concerned that "here is George Bush, a man who had climbed the ladder

to get his party's nomination, had served as an ambassa-
dor to China, had been head of the CIA, he was Mr.
Competent compared to Mr. What?" his running mate.

So that is why I asked George Bush about that part of
the Constitution which provides for, "If, at the time fixed
for the beginning of the term of the president, the president-elect shall have died, the vice president-elect shall
become president." And the thrust of my question was,
"How could you do this? And having done it, are you at
peace with Dan Quayle in that position?"

Both questions were asked with the intent of making
them relevant to issues in the campaign. There was nothing whimsical about either of those questions. I knew that
both questions had to be personal. The one to Dukakis had
to be personal. They had to be personal if they were to
pierce the campaign body armor.

*So a factor in phrasing the question was the aim of
eliciting a response that was more than just words, a
reaction that we would see visually?*

Yes. That's all part of it. Television is an omnipresent
medium.

Did you have any idea of how Dukakis would react?

I had no idea before asking the question how he would
react. I was concerned that the question might seem so
utterly soft, that he would handle it so comfortably and so
assuringly and so convincingly that in retrospect critics
might say, "Well, Shaw asked him the softest of questions
and Dukakis hit it out of the park." That was one of my
concerns. After a while I became so frustrated with trying
to anticipate reaction—my utter belief in journalistic prin-
ciples saved me. At one point I said, "Wait a minute, I'm a
reporter. To hell with critics and people's perceptions. I
have got to ask the best question I can formulate. That is
my responsibility." The rest of it was easy for me.

When I asked the question, I was simply stunned that Governor Dukakis did not pause and reflect on the words in the question. I had barely asked the question and his response was "No, Bernard" and he started in with his response to my question. That surprised me. And you know that after the debate when he walked off stage, his campaign manager was in the wings, and the first thing Dukakis said to him was "I blew it."

When you thought, "This question might be perceived as being too soft," what convinced you to go ahead with the question?

Reminding myself that I am first and foremost a journalist, and my concern must not be how critics will react to my question. I'm not in the business of pleasing anybody. It is not my role to be popular.

Did Dukakis's response say anything to you about his character and his ability to lead the country?

I didn't make those kinds of judgments. And as moderator you are doing two to four to five things at once, when you're moderating a presidential debate. So I did not have time to evaluate how he responded. I just remember thinking as he launched into his response, without giving it due thought . . . I remember thinking, "Governor . . . that's not the right response."

Looking back now four years later, did Dukakis's response indicate something about his abilities to you?

It would be unfair to him to extrapolate from his response to that question.

There's debate as to whether his response genuinely reflected on his ability to lead the country. Some feel, "He got shafted. It was unfair for the public to judge him on that response." The other side is "No. This showed a piece of Dukakis that was very important." What do you think?

I think it was very important to voters trying to make a judgment. It was a window; he opened a window on his character and his personality—more his personality than his character. But, I pull back from making any sweeping judgments about his ability to lead a nation based solely on his response to my question. I just point out to people, it wasn't the question that did in Michael Dukakis; it was Dukakis's answer. Since when did a question even approach defeating a candidate?

When you say it was more of a window on his personality than his character, what do you mean?

Personality is the impression people get of a politician— what that politician projects. And again, in all of our polling data, people did not doubt Governor Dukakis's administrative abilities. But they did not get anything from his personality. They didn't feel that they were seeing or hearing the kind of real, or imaginary, person that they tend to want to react to when considering a president.

Character is something much deeper; character involves ethics and everything else. I would pull back abruptly from making character judgments just because of the way he responded to that question. I'm a reporter, not a psychiatrist. I still get mail from people who either approve strongly or disapprove mightily of that question. I find interesting that body of opinion which still exists which is aghast that I would ask that question, especially "being a Democrat." People assumed that I'm a Democrat. Many of them assumed I'm a Democrat because I'm an African-American, because my skin is black.

Then there is another body of opinion that applauded me because they assume I was a Republican. I actually had a man interrupt a dinner with my family in the dining room of a hotel restaurant in Washington and say, "I'm a Republican, and I just want to thank you for what you did." I was appalled. Anger just rushed through my body.

Finally he left and a few minutes afterwards, a waitress came over with a chilled bottle of champagne and she said, "The man at the other table before he left asked that this be brought to you." "I cannot accept that; I will not accept that" were my words to the waitress. So I just wanted to give you a feel for the pendulum on this . . . by the way, I'm neither a Democrat nor a Republican.

Dukakis's response was aired repeatedly in '88 and in '92. Do you think the news media gave it too much play?

I think, first of all, that was a signal moment in American politics, in an American presidential campaign. That was one of the signal moments of the '88 campaign, there's no denying that. I debate whether or not that caused him to lose the election, especially when you consider the record of how he was doing in the polls. That was a factor, but I don't know whether that was the consummate decider. As to people saying that the media overplayed it, I look at it differently.

People forget that the news industry is omnipresent in our society, because this is the information age.

Whether it's a little girl falling down a well or Dukakis responding to a question, when the news media cover it as a story, it's going to get widespread play. And the volume and intensity and the density of that coverage are unavoidable. Tell me, what newspaper is going to ignore a story because CNN covered it ad nauseam the night before?

What do you say to the criticism that we are too emotional about our presidents, that we should choose our presidents more along the lines of their stances on specific issues?

Oh, I think that's too cerebral [laughing]! Politics is very basic and very emotional. Americans have a certain pre-conceived idea of what their president is supposed to represent, and those preconceptions are contradictory. We want our president to be "one of the boys," but not one of the boys. We want our president to be like "the guy next door"; we want to be able to like him. But how can a president be the guy next door when in all likelihood the president is in the top 1 percent economic bracket to begin with? We want to be able to love our president, respect our president, but yet we also want to hold him or her to a higher standard and I don't know that that's fully realistic.

So in general, what would your goals be when interviewing a presidential candidate in depth? What would you like it to reveal?

My interview would be a mix, because it would be an effort to enable viewers watching and listening to the interview to learn as much as the candidate would be willing to share with the viewer. Every question asked that candidate would have the sole intent of gaining insight and information. There would be no effort to surprise, to embarrass, to embellish on that candidate and what she or he might stand for.

I know that much of the interview would be very issues driven, but I also know that I would ask questions which I hope would reveal a feel for the candidate, an emotional feel for the candidate. And in the process of doing that kind of interview, some critics would say that some questions were off the wall and unfair, too tough, too personal, too bland, too predictable. There would always be grounds for anyone to express a supporting or critical view because that's the way opinions are. I certainly would not be doing the interview to please anyone, least of all the candidate.

NOTE

1. Goldman, Peter, and Mathews, Tom, *The Quest for the Presidency: 1988* (New York: Simon and Schuster, 1989), p. 392.

9

TOM BROKAW

Tom Brokaw is the Anchor and Managing Editor of *NBC Nightly News*.

When Tom Brokaw covered the White House for NBC News he would check the White House visitor lists for out-of-town vistors and track them down at their hotels to ask them what was being talked about "back home." When he'd arrived in Washington in 1973 to take on the White House beat, Washington struck Brokaw the way it strikes many Americans—exciting, but insular. Brokaw grew up in the small town of Yankton, South Dakota, and throughout his career, as he worked his way up from a reporter for a small TV station in Nebraska to anchor for a major network, staying in touch with his roots has always been on his mind.

Like politicians, the more successful journalists become, the tighter an atmosphere of deference encircles them. Add to that celebrity status, a pressure-packed schedule, and a multimillion-dollar salary and even the most clear-headed and well-intentioned can become insulated. Resisting that kind of insulation has been one of Brokaw's main concerns throughout his career. For him the world of Washington politics and journalism has always been double-edged: "I love Washington and I love the people who live there for all the reasons that they were attracted there—they're bright and they care about what's going on. But I do think it can be a real narcotic."

Brokaw took his first job as a reporter in 1963 at KMTV, a small television station in Omaha, Nebraska. In 1965 he became an anchor for the NBC affilate in Atlanta and then in 1966 signed on as news anchor for KNBC-TV in Los Angeles. When he arrived, Richard Threlkeld, then a CBS correspondent, pegged Brokaw as "just a pretty face."[1] But however "blow-dried" Brokaw may have seemed to some of his peers, he countered the impression with his coverage of California politics at that time—Reagan's defeat of incumbent Governor Edmund G. "Pat" Brown, the antiwar movement, Robert Kennedy's assassination in 1968.

Brokaw moved up to White House correspondent for NBC in 1973, landing in the aggressive White House press room just as it was teetering on the brink of Watergate. Then in 1976 NBC management was scrambling to put together a pair of new faces to revive the *Today* show's sagging ratings and after a lengthy courtship Brokaw signed a five-year contract to co-anchor the morning news show.

Brokaw's stint on *Today* was both an asset and a stigma. *Today* showcased his talent for ad-libbing and his youthful, appealing personality, yet it reinforced the impression that because his temperament was so suitable to television, he wasn't a serious journalist. In retrospect the stigma would lose its bite. Brokaw's "other half" on *Today* was an anchor who would overcome similar hurdles, having once been dubbed by a media critic as having the "IQ of canteloupe": Jane Pauley.

In 1982, NBC was dogged by low ratings and wanted to replace their nightly news anchor, John Chancellor. After much wheeling and dealing, Brokaw signed a seven-year,

$18 million contract to co-anchor *NBC Nightly News* with Roger Mudd.

The first few years were especially tumultuous. Amid fiscal cutbacks, morale was down and the news division lost an estimated $70 million. In a much criticized gesture, NBC management dropped Mudd from the team in 1983. It was a triumph of image over substance, critics said, youth and good looks over credibility and experience. But over time, Brokaw countered the criticism that he lacked serious journalistic credentials and NBC's ratings improved.

After the 1988 election, Brokaw shared the view that campaign coverage needed to undergo serious reform, that the networks were too vulnerable to handlers, and that the coverage should focus more on the issues that concerned ordinary Americans. In 1992 more NBC correspondents were "off the campaign bus" and out "in the country" reporting on issues, and scrutiny of campaign ads was tightened. NBC News also partnered up with PBS's *Mac-Neil / Lehrer NewsHour* to cover the conventions. The deal was in part an effort to pool financial and technical resources, but it provided more issue-oriented coverage, combining NBC's convention-floor coverage with *Mac-Neil / Lehrer's* fleet of commentators.

When you prepared for the '92 presidential campaign, what was most important to you in planning the coverage?

The foremost lessons in the minds of everyone were the failures of 1988. We were determined to kind of regain control of our senses, regain control [laughing] of the process of press coverage. In 1988 there was a kind of consensus that we had surrendered too much of our judgment and had been manipulated too skillfully by the handlers in the two campaigns, that we kind of played into their hands.

As much as anything in '88 we failed to get at the real issues of the campaign separate from the campaign appearances. So in '92 one of the operating rules we had at NBC was that we would not put our primary people "on the bus," so to speak. We would have them apart from the travel apparatus of the campaign, so that they could have a broader and more clear-headed view of what was at stake. I think what had begun to happen in too many campaigns was that the manipulation in the confined area of a campaign airplane or the traveling campaign press just got wildly out of control.

So you were trying to look at things more in terms of the condition of the country and then the campaign, instead of the other way around?

It wasn't that we didn't connect the two of them. We always understood the synergy between what a candidate was saying and what the country was concerned about. But we felt that to strike the appropriate balance it was important not to have our primary people just worrying about "where the body was that day."

So that was uppermost in our minds. I went into the '92 campaign determined to keep it as focused as much as possible on the issues (and) to raise television and radio, and for that matter, print advertising on the part of the campaigns to a primary issue deserving of coverage.

What did you do differently as far as advertisements were concerned?

We assigned somebody to them and did series of tests in which we would ask—Is the ad true? Is it contextual? Is it relevant to the race? And when we broadcast an excerpt from a commercial we weren't just giving one of the campaigns more commercial time we would always put the commercial inside a television set and make it very clear that it was a commercial.

So you felt that some commercials were getting repeated by newscasts in '88?

We just got behind the curve in '88—we really were not as vigilant as we needed to have been. I think everybody agreed to that. That was kind of a universal sentiment coming out of the '88 campaign was that we pedaled, but not hard enough. Some of what happened as well in '88 was skewed of course by the Gary Hart episode.

Do you think the amount of coverage of the Hart episode was justified?

Well I think it helped create what can only be described as the kind of "feeding frenzy syndrome" of current campaign coverage. That was such an unusual and slightly hysterical time. But I believe that Gary Hart deserved all that attention. That is not to say that I can defend every story about it, but I think in the broad context it was an issue worth covering. It went to judgment. It went to character. Also there is a change in our attitudes about the treatment of women in this country on the part of men. The era of politicians just kind of "having their way" if you will, the double standard about women, had come to an end before '88. And I thought it was reflected in that campaign.

I know for a fact that there were members of Hart's campaign who'd gone to work for him with at least the tacit understanding that those behavior patterns on his part were over. Because they were unsettled by the treatment of his wife and the kind of duplicity of his life.

When the Gennifer Flowers story broke, what were your greatest concerns about covering it?

My greatest concern was that we would blow it out of proportion. We kept saying to ourselves here, "What's the relevance?" It was well known that Clinton had "strayed" from his marriage—I guess that's the best way to describe that . . . it was well known within political circles. Had Clinton changed his ways? All the evidence was that he had. Was he being hypocritical about it? No. He'd raised the issue in that original Washington meeting with the press corps.

But then when Flowers—listen, it could have been for *Foreign Affairs* quarterly as well for the *Enquirer* or the *Sun* or anybody else—when she went as public as she did, it was impossible to ignore. Then when we did cover it, we tried to keep it constantly in perspective. And all three of the networks, I think, gave it maybe one or two nights' attention.

What do you say to the view that the Flowers coverage was just another example of how the networks let the tabloids set their standards?

What I say is that the issue—if not Gennifer Flowers by name—had been of enormous concern to the Clinton campaign almost from the get-go. In fact before he officially declared his candidacy, Clinton was taking soundings in New York and right off the bat I was hearing that Clinton was worried about a period in his personal life when he'd strayed from his marriage and that it was going to come out in some fashion. So we knew that it was a legitimate concern within the campaign and that, by admission of even people who knew him well, it in fact was true.

I also happen to believe that to a certain degree these are relevant issues. That we do elect presidents not just for their positions on foreign policy or how they're going to reform health care. But they are reflections of who we are and what we stand for and what we value.

And I think you should examine not just the fact that we covered the Gennifer Flowers story, but the manner in which we covered it. We did it fairly; we did put it in context. We did exercise judgment and it was done with restraint. We wrestled with it around here. And there are lots of other things that came up that we didn't cover just because they were out there in the air.

If you compare the Flowers story to Hart's Donna Rice episode, what differences do you see regarding the candidates' character?

There'd always been the questions about "who is Gary Hart?" There'd always been a question about "is he honest in describing himself? Does he have an honest evaluation of who he is?" And you recall the Friday before the Donna Rice episode broke Hart said, "You can follow me" and that "there was absolutely nothing to these stories." Clinton never engaged in that.

It raised questions about character as much as anything. I think it's a real issue. I think the difference between Bill Clinton and Gary Hart was the hypocrisy question. Gary Hart had said, "It's over. I'm not doing it anymore. You can follow me around." He was capital "P" pious about the issue, and at the same time, he had Donna Rice staying at his house! That's a quantum difference.

Do you think there was a sentiment in the press that Clinton was one of the most viable Democratic candidates in years and that because of that the press backed off the Flowers story?

No. He had a couple people who fell in love with him. But not everybody. To his credit Clinton had better skills than people had seen for a while. That's true. He was well-versed in a wide range of subjects, he was able to articulate them, he was well organized, he knew where he wanted to get to. I would remind you that four years earlier, Bruce Babitt had a sweetheart relationship with some of the American press.

Clinton underwent an image makeover during '92—his rhetoric became more populist; he spoke more about his family. Do you think that makeover was a distortion?

No. I'd been following him a long time, well before he became a presidential candidate. When I was doing the *Today* show I used him as part of a little "repertory company" that I kept around the country and that I could call on. So I had known about who Bill was and where he came from and what his interests were. And I thought what I saw in the campaign was pretty much what I knew about him.

When a guy comes out of Yale and is bright and is identified as a Yale Law School graduate and Georgetown graduate and Rhodes Scholar, any campaign is going to say, "Hey, wait a minute, that's only a half of it, or a third of it. There's this other life that he has." And Clinton didn't get elected in Arkansas for five terms by being some kind of an ivory-tower elitist. One of the reasons he got elected in Arkansas is that he spoke the language, he knew the back roads of that place.

You once said about Reagan in an interview that there were "vast gaps" between his beliefs and what average Americans go through. Of all the presidential candidates you've interviewed, who seemed the least insulated from ordinary life by their campaign or the White House?

You know the name that springs almost . . . quickly to mind is Fritz Mondale. It has to do with his kind of "Methodist minister's son" background—he never really had access to money, he lived a pretty plain life in Washington. . . . And he represented a state in which they keep you pretty close to the ground. I think both those guys from Minnesota, Hubert Humphrey and Fritz, were both pretty much in touch with how the rest of the country lives.

I guess my regional bias is showing . . . I also feel that way about Bob Dole. I come from that part of the world and I know those guys and they're smart and tough and more vulnerable than they let on [laughing]. They really are. When I see Dole, he'll make some comment about South Dakota—he always remembers that that's where I'm from, and knows my roots and hooks into that right away. And it's common ground to us, and I do think it's helpful to know people in Russell, Kansas.

Reagan hadn't touched ground in forty years. But I also believe that he had an uncanny ability to—if not experience it firsthand—to, in a case-by-case basis, identify with people. If you took Reagan into a bar in Southy, he was at ease instantly. It was never forced for him like it would be for George Bush—he would never order a "Courvoisier" [laughing]. I don't think it was just acting, I think Reagan was often very comfortable around people. One of his best friends when he was governor was the highway patrolman who drove him all those years, an old guy by the name of Barney who worked up at the ranch with him.

An interesting thing about Robert Kennedy . . . he did come from a life of privilege and he was insulated from what almost everyone else in the world goes through, but he made *an effort* to find out. And it was less "intellectual growth" than it was a visceral, emotional thing. That every time he got exposed to it, he learned from it. He just didn't walk away from it.

He was often not a very pleasant man to deal with, Bobby. He was a man of very strong judgment. And he would come at you in a very direct, confrontational kind of way. But what would happen is that he was constantly taking in information, not just sending it out. And of all the politicians that I've known and watched for a long, long time—he more than any of the rest of them saw it as an organic experience. You know, he started it at one level and worked his way "down" in a manner of speaking, to get in touch with people. It's really true that he grew, that he changed.

Do you think that Bush got too insulated and that it was one of the reasons he lost in '92?

I think even his friends will tell you that (A) he was very late to recognize the frustration in the land; (B) there was chaotic organization of his campaign; (C) the Republican National Convention, which was to be the "great launching pad," was a disaster.

Do you think talk shows and town halls may help keep Clinton from getting too insulated?

To a certain degree. I think he's got better political antennae than George Bush did.

What do you say to the charge that the networks failed to adequately cover the realities brought on by supply-side economics during Reagan's tenure?

There was a lot of criticism of supply-side economics. But you know it's always hard to say, when things seem to be going good, that "Armageddon is coming" [laughing] and get people to respond to it. I was just talking last night to a friend of mine here, about a very good documentary that we did in the mid-eighties called *Wall Street, Money, Greed and Power*. And that was all about the eighties; that was all about the "runaway train" thing.

I think the press got the word out to a fair degree. I think that if you go back and look at the whole supply-side economic coverage, there was a lot of skepticism about it. There were lots of questions that were raised about it. I think we did a better job in '92 than we've done in the past, because it was "the issue" this time and there were consequences that people started having to start to deal with that were enormous.

Do you think the increased influence of talk shows like Donahue *and* Larry King Live *improves the process?*

I'm on the twentieth Century Fund committee that's look-ing at campaign coverage, and some of my colleagues are outraged by the place that Larry King and Donahue hold. I can't get over this. I mean, my God! Who are we to say that they shouldn't have an opportunity to interview the presidential candidates and that we won't learn some-thing from it? Plus, the candidates' appearances on those kinds of programs brought that many more people into the political arena in America, which I think is good.

There was an enormous amount of coverage this time. Very good debates—there were debates in all the prima-ries with very pointed, specific questions. There were the *Today* show interviews, and *CBS Morning News* and *Good Morning America* all did very specific, issue-oriented in-terviews. And King and Donahue and the others were part of all of that.

Do you think Ross Perot's candidacy flourished because of talk shows, that he couldn't have survived in the older campaign environment in which traditional journalists were the primary gatekeepers?

Baloney. Look at George Wallace. We've had lots of these guys along the years—third-party candidates who've got-ten lots of attention.

Has there ever been a time that you felt the quality of press coverage affected the outcome of a presidential elec-tion?

I don't think it ever affected the outcome. I do think that, for example, in '64 Lyndon Johnson had much different coverage than Barry Goldwater did. Much, much differ-ent. As I witnessed it—and I was not on the bus, but I was working in Omaha and I would catch Johnson on the midwestern tours and so on. There would be a much more sympathetic press traveling with Lyndon than was traveling with Barry Goldwater.

There was much talk that the press lightened up on Reagan after having chewed the Carter presidency to pieces. Do you think the press went lighter on Reagan than they did Carter?

I think that Jimmy Carter in his tenure as president was the victim of his own naïveté. I don't know whether the president himself feels this way but I think the people who were around him in retrospect don't feel that they were unnecessarily "roughed up" by the press. I think if he were the man then that he is today, that he would have been a stronger candidate.

What is the difference between him now and then?

I think he's got more political sophistication, if you will. I think he probably has learned something about the economy. I do think that everybody gets a honeymoon. And I think that Reagan got a honeymoon; he had a landslide election. The country was saying, "This is what we'd like to see for a while."

I remember on the *Today* show we did a couple of very long special editions in which we covered people who were going to become in effect victims of the Reagan cutback. We got a hell of a lot of criticism for it, but we felt it was necessary to do that.

Looking back at Carter's presidency, why do you think things went so badly?

Well, there were some things that were out of control for him. The Iranian hostages was a big piece of it; it seemed that we were powerless. He seemed not equipped to handle the economy. And then just in the administration of his office—they did not use the word "malaise" in his speech, but when he went "on to the mountaintop" to try to figure out [laughing] what he in effect was saying was wrong with the country—when the country had already figured out what was wrong with Jimmy Carter. He never seemed strong and commanding to a lot of people.

And what worked for Reagan is that he said, "I want to restore the lustre of the presidency." We can have all these intellectual debates about the "imperial presidency," but it does occupy a special place in the minds and hearts of most Americans, and Reagan knew how to seize on that.

Do you think Carter was naïve about the symbolism of the presidency?

I think to some degree. It worked so well for him in the campaign that he just extended it too long. When he came along in '76, the country was ready for a voice from the outside and a kind of populist approach. Because after all we were dealing with the hangover of Watergate and what I think a lot of Americans believed was that the antidote to Watergate was to go well outside the beltway.

And Jimmy Carter used all those expressions like "I will never lie to you" and he seemed to be much more "of the people" than Gerald Ford, who had spent most of his adult life in Washington. But then at some point you have to switch gears, as Bill Clinton has been learning, and you have to become presidential. People want someone who serves in that office to have stature, to have bearing, to be just a little bit above the rest of us. Because it's an office they want to look up to and that can be useful to a president—it's a commanding position.

What do you think went wrong when Clinton made the transition from the '92 campaign to the White House?

My own guess based on close witness is that what happened is that his campaign had been so difficult— through the whole Gennifer Flowers thing, you know, he rose from the dead nine times or something—he developed a campaign momentum and by the time the election was over and they got back down to Little Rock they never turned off the campaign machinery and started up the White House machinery.

And so by the time he arrived in Washington it was like an extension of the campaign. And his staff will say to you now that they made grievous errors in the interim between November and January 20, in how they organized themselves in Little Rock without having a Chief of Staff until the very end, how they set their priorities. They'd been so concentrated on the campaign right to the last gasp that they hadn't thought very carefully about who they wanted in office and under what circumstances.

I rode with him partly on that last Sunday from Monticello up toward Washington before the Inauguration and I just had the impression of a guy who was enormously relieved to be out of Little Rock and trying to figure out what he was going to do when he got to Washington.

How much of an influence do you think David Gergen has had?

I think a fair amount. I've been a student of the White House organization—in fact in August of '92 I talked one summer night in Little Rock to Stephanopoulos, saying that whether it's a Republican or a Democrat who wins, one of the real truisms that Al Haig ever shared with me was no one has a full appreciation of how complex the White House machinery is until you arrive there. It comes in over the transom and under the door and through the windows twenty-four hours a day—a wide range of issues, all manner of subjects that require decisions "now" and have enormous consequences. And George—very bright guy—looked at me, and said, "God. That's absolutely true." And then they got there and they simply weren't prepared. . . . Gergen had been there before. He went in and said, "These are some easy things that you can do." I'll tell you something; it helps to have spent time in Washington.

Do you think it's true that in some senses we can't really figure out what kind of a leader a candidate is going to be—that you really can't predict?

To some degree I think that's true. . . . I think that there are some telltale signs, based on their past record, based on their conduct in the course of a campaign. I mean, Reagan ran his presidency pretty much the way he ran his campaign [laughing]. He kind of appeared for the ceremonial occasions.

NOTE

1. Goldberg, Gerald Jay, and Goldberg, Robert, *Anchors: Brokaw, Jennings, and Rather, and the Evening News* (New York: Birch Lane Press, 1990), p. 52.

10

ROGER ROSENBLATT

Roger Rosenblatt is a contributing editor and essayist for the *MacNeil/Lehrer NewsHour, The New Republic, The New York Times Magazine, Vanity Fair, Men's Journal,* and *Family Circle,* and Editor-in-Chief of *The Columbia Journalism Review.*

He was watching a news report on the Iran-Iraq war when he saw an Iraqi child, three or four years old, standing in the rubble of a bombed-out area. "It was just a child crying because of the noise and the chaos caused by the bombs. . . . Three words just came into my mind, 'Children of War.' "

The next day Roger Rosenblatt took an idea to his editor at *Time* magazine for a series of articles on children in countries besieged by war. The project would take him around the globe, to Belfast, Israel, Lebanon, Cambodia, and Vietnam, to document the lives of children in countries ravaged by war. The stories of these children, the words and images which Rosenblatt sent back, showed the profoundly human dimension of war—stories of enormous devastation, but also hope.

Published by *Time* in 1982, the articles formed the basis for Rosenblatt's book, *Children of War*, and set the tone for his work to come. The human face of politics has been Rosenblatt's trade in force. Be it presidential politics or specific issues, such as abortion or capital punishment, Rosenblatt brings to his subjects a distinct reflectiveness—an unusually acute sense for the human interior and the stark realities which are the consequences of politics.

When Rosenblatt began his travels for the *Children of War* articles, he had never done any reporting, nor had he traveled widely. He began his career in journalism as the Literary Editor for *The New Republic* in 1975. A year later he became a columnist and member of the editorial board of *The Washington Post* and in 1980 joined *Time* magazine as an essayist and Senior Writer.

In 1982 the *MacNeil/Lehrer NewsHour*, then just spreading its wings, approached Rosenblatt to read one of his essays on the air. The first broadcast essay was a success and *MacNeil/Lehrer* asked Rosenblatt to sign on as a regular essayist. What resulted was a new journalistic form: the essay as a visual narrative. For over ten years Rosenblatt's essays have punctuated *MacNeil/Lehrer*'s broadcasts and numerous other columnists and editors now contribute essays in the same form.

Several times a month Rosenblatt will write an essay, a few paragraphs in length, and send it to his producers at *MacNeil/Lehrer*, who then develop a sequence of pictures and graphics for the essay. Rosenblatt will read the whole essay on a prompter and in the final edit he will appear two or three times, the rest of the tape serving as voice-over for the pictures. Because of the speed at which they work, Rosenblatt never sees the final essay until it's broadcast.

In television reporting images often create the skeleton for a story. In the case of Rosenblatt's *MacNeil/Lehrer* essays, the words—the ideas, emotions, facts, and insights—come first. Then the images are tailored to the narrative to create the final essay. The result? Visual narratives with the fluency of writing, delivered in short form, yet still imbued with the mysterious undertow of revelation found in the works of great writers.

Rosenblatt has written over three hundred TV essays in the ten-plus years *MacNeil / Lehrer* has been on the air. In addition to serving as essayist and editor for *Time*, *The New Republic*, *The Washington Post*, and *U.S. News and World Report*, he has served as columnist and Editor-at-Large for *Life* magazine. He currently is a contributing editor and essayist for *Family Circle, Men's Journal, The New Republic, The New York Times Magazine*, and *Vanity Fair* and is the Editor-in-Chief of the *Columbia Journalism Review*. Since authoring *Children of War*, he has written several books: *Witness: The World Since Hiroshima, Life Itself: Abortion in the American Mind*, and most recently, *The Man in the Water*, a collection of stories and essays.

Do you ever consider what you do "objective reporting"?

It's very hard to do objective reporting for me. I want to humanize the subject—to bring, not necessarily a humanitarian, but a humanistic perspective to issues that are often relegated to the social sciences. I try to talk about politics in terms of ethics and personality and character, rather than in terms of "who's going to win what district" and so forth. There are those who spend their lives predicting outcomes, and they're much better equipped to write about that than I am. I write about politics as a human endeavor.

Most of the essays I do for *MacNeil / Lehrer* are general essays—that is, they don't take a particular side; they try to explore a phenomenon. Of course I start from a definite position by saying up front, "OK, I'm one of these guys who is against prayer in public schools, but that's not what this essay is about. This essay's about what it means to pray in public schools." Similiarly with gun control, or abortion or capital punishment or any of the other large issues. I start off saying, in effect, "I'm one of the people for or against your point of view, but this essay's going to try to do something else." The essay deals much more with perspective than opinion. The opinion is merely the starting point.

I think that the effort to be objective ought not to be confused with the effort to be fair. The idea of trying to be objective is not as interesting to me as the idea of being fair—showing as much as one can of all things that happen, even though you're pretty sure that at the end of it you'll wind up saying, "Here is the person you should feel sorry for, here's the side that is right, here's the side that is wrong."

What do you say to the view that the networks' standard of objectivity is really a "thin veil for protecting the status quo" and that this was especially the case during the Reagan era?

It's really hard to know. Television reporting generally is weak, very weak. For one thing there's the dissonance between words and images. This others have spoken about, but I know it from my own essays for *MacNeil / Lehrer*. If my essay talked about ducks and I showed you a picture of a chicken, you would think that the essay was about chickens. And the picture so dominates the intellectual sense of any piece on television that all one really has to do is to arrange an event where the picture gives the desired message. It doesn't matter what anybody says.

It's easy to arrange your words; it's much harder to arrange pictures on television that suit the words. You can find a picture of a president waving to a cheering crowd, but you can't find a picture of a president being stupid. If you're going to say he's been stupid or crooked or wrong or narrow or mean-spirited or acting against the public good, you can't find a picture to go along with that. There is no picture of Reagan cutting back on the lunch programs in schools, for example, because it's not a visual act; there's no picture of Reagan not helping the teenagers in programs that were established by Jimmy Carter and by the Great Society of Johnson before that. Certain important acts are simply not visual. There is no picture of Reagan deciding to give tax breaks to big business, but there *is* a picture of Reagan invading Grenada.

And then there's the question of "What is a story?" in politics. Is the story "How the president wants to try to pass a bill" or "How hard it will be to get something like health care or NAFTA through Congress"? Is that the story? Or is the story "What does health care *mean* in America? How will universal health care change American life?" I think the first kind of story lends itself better to political reporting in general. It's easier. The second kind is more difficult, and there are no pictures to go with it.

I also think that most people in television have no practice in print, and therefore do not have practice in the medium which teaches you what it is you really are thinking. It's not that they're unintelligent—I know many of these people; they're highly intelligent. And some of them are good writers. But they don't think like writers.

Writers really learn what they think as they write. Paragraph follows paragraph and they start to clarify that swamp and chaos in their minds into definite sentences with definite punctuation. And they suddenly realize what they've believed all along. They find their order.

That process doesn't occur in television. To the contrary, people ask, "What happened today?" And then they write the story of what happened and they show pictures of it. But a TV story doesn't have any of the self-discovery that a written story provides.

When you are writing your essays for MacNeil/Lehrer, *are you thinking in a visual way?*

When I do, I'm a goner. When I start to think, "What pictures would go with this?" the writing gets worse and worse. I'm coming out with a collection of my writing. I've written over a thousand things in the eighteen-plus years I've been in journalism. Of those maybe three hundred are *MacNeil/Lehrer* essays. Not a single television essay am I including in the book, because they do not hold up as writing.

I think the best of my *MacNeil/Lehrer* essays are fair writing and I think the worst of them are bad. Where they get bad is when I start to anticipate the image, instead of creating it in my mind. In other words, an image ought to be the embodiment of thought or the product of thought. It ought not to be something that one leaps toward before thought.

And if you do that, if you lurch forward "before thought" prematurely, what happens?

You lose inventiveness. You lose originality. For example, I'm writing about the thirtieth anniversary of the Kennedy assassination, and I want to put it in a historical context— "so let's think about how many other presidents were assassinated and get pictures of them." So I start to think of McKinley and the Reagan shooting and Lincoln and so forth. Now that's all too easy! In other words, I'm thinking from the outside, not the inside, of a subject.

I should think entirely from the inside. If it turns out to be too abstract, let the producers worry about it; let them worry about making it pictorial. That's not my business. A writer's business is to come up with the heart of the matter.

Do you think that some talk shows take the dissonance between words and images to the extreme and thus are more vulnerable to manipulation by candidates?

Yes. There's no question that when the candidates started to use Larry King and other talk-show hosts, they were taking full advantage of the idea that *they* are the image, *they* are the message. And they were being asked questions by people who are not interested in belittling, criticizing, or finding fault with or fissures in their lines of thought.

If a talk show like Larry King's has a lot of influence on a campaign, should certain standards be exercised in terms of how a candidate is questioned?

I'm not sure I know the answer to that question. I don't think that Larry King ought to feel obliged to become Bryant Gumble—I think that Gumble is a great political interviewer, by the way. I think that Larry King serves a purpose in being trusted by great and powerful people to bring their message across. I think what he does is really provide a medium, a mouthpiece.

But if he does that, then others ought to be waiting to be much more critical or much more angled in their approach to the issues. Because if that's all that television ever did—that is, just to provide the candidates with an opportunity of looking as good as they can—then that wouldn't be journalism.

What do you say to the view that such passivity is irresponsible because it allows attacks and innuendo to get wide play without being challenged?

Well, Larry King doesn't seem to me to be practiced in the work of journalism. I think he's much more practiced in the encouragement of light conversation. Before Ross Perot found his happy home on the *Larry King* show, I don't think the Larry King show had many politicians finding their proper niche there. I think he had mostly entertainers. George Bush found that he could look his best on *Larry King*. But if Bush got away with something on the *Larry King* show, he sure didn't get away with the same thing in an interview with Robin MacNeil in 1992. I'm persuaded that that interview lost the election for George Bush.

It was the most revealing political interview I've ever seen on television. If it had been translated to print it would have been no less effective. Bush was given an opportunity to shine in the context of extremely difficult questions. If he had come out of that experience well, people would have looked on Bush entirely differently—as somebody who really was capable of running the country for four more years and was educated by the experience of the first four years. Instead he either had no answers or poor answers to questions that would be asked of anybody in his position.

I remember Robin telling me afterwards that Bush's people called up in a fury that he, Robin, had violated the agreement of what the subject matter of the interview was to be. Well this simply was untrue; there was no agreement as to what the subject matter was. It wasn't as if Robin had revealed that Bush had been sleeping with a sheep in a hotel in Connecticut. There was nothing that ought to have come as a surprise. That was the thing about the interview, Bush seemed shocked to be asked things that any presidential candidate would have expected to be asked.

But why was this particular interview so striking?

Robin was relentless. There was question after question after question about things that had to do with the Gulf War, things that had to do with domestic programs, things that pertained to the dissolution of the Soviet Union, and so forth. I had never seen them marshaled in one place. In other words, if you wanted one place to see the candidate good or bad, that interview was it.

MacNeil/Lehrer is watched by about five million people. That night the audience might have been a little larger because the president was on. My opinion is that that interview, more than anything else, certainly more than anything positive that Clinton did, lost the election for Bush. Because Bush *lost* the election; it wasn't that

Clinton won the election. He was unable to rise to an occasion that was within the normal expectations of a president.

Robin could have done this in print and had the same effect. But to see it. My God, to see it! And there it comes back to the Larry King show. Let's say I get a haircut and really look as good as I can, and smile and everything—"tanned and rested" as they say of Nixon. And I go on and just give my point of view; the cooperation of the image and the words works entirely in my favor. If, on the other hand, I create exactly the same circumstances but I am not able to talk, and I look angry and confused and really lost—there it works entirely against me. So you have a very big gamble taking place on television. If you have Larry King you have a good chance of looking fine. If you have Robin MacNeil you've got to know what you're talking about.

What do you think of the view that Ross Perot's political success is one of the best arguments for traditional journalistic practices?

I think he's certainly a good argument for traditional journalistic forms. He's not going to choose to be interviewed by Robin MacNeil; he's going to choose to be interviewed by Larry King. And who could blame him? Larry King's doing his job and Perot is taking advantage of that context. But then it becomes incumbent on other journalists, not necessarily in television, to be very hard with Ross Perot.

Every presidential campaign television journalism is criticized for obssessing on personal character and yet there's a lot of public interest in it. As a nation, are we overinvested in issues of personal character?

I have a different view of this. My view is that we don't know enough about character, while pretending to know everything. In other words, if you're going to be in for a nickel, why not be in for a million? Would you want your character to be defined by the fact that you were or were not cheating on your husband or your wife? Would you want your character to be defined by some sexual peccadillo or some earlier social nonsense or the fact that you dated a movie star or did not?

In other words, all of these things are claimed to be signals of character, and they certainly may be. But they also may be small change. Take Bill Clinton. His character was called into question by the Gennifer Flowers episode. Why isn't his character being called into question when he is for capital punishment? Why wasn't his character called into question for his ordinance against flag burning in Arkansas? Why are we defining character by the elements that go into tabloids and gossip, when we know perfectly well that we would never stand for anybody defining our character in such terms?

I think people do want to know what the character of a president is—and I think they ought to know. And I think it's about the only thing they *can* know, frankly, in a political campaign. That is, there are maybe half a dozen issues, two of them are related to foreign affairs—therefore nobody pays attention to them—four of them are domestic and one of those is the economy. Everyone pays attention to that, but everything else is just chatter.

Really the issues are the last things that anyone really gets a sense of in candidates, unless you have the oddity of a Ronald Reagan, who comes along every once in a while and says, "I just represent an entirely different point of view." But that rarely happens.

So what do you personally look for in a presidential candidate?

I want character defined in a generous and wide way. In other words, when I go back to Bill Clinton, who purports to have liberal views and in fact does have many of them—

I want to know why he is for capital punishment. That to me would reveal an element of character. Why would he go back to personally witness an execution in his state? What statement is he making by that? That to me is far more interesting than whether he's spent a wild and sweaty night with Gennifer Flowers. Right now sex is the whole story of character. You could have a guy who's the worst son of a bitch on earth, and because he never cheated on his wife, he looks moral.

A lot of journalists were unsettled by how much Clinton lied about his past—about dodging the draft, smoking marijuana, and the Gennifer Flowers story. They felt he was "too smooth." How did it strike you?

Well, he was hardly smooth. I mean, a smooth person would have said, "I smoked marijuana and I was a member of my generation—forget it!" And people would have said, "Yeah, sure." It was the fact that he said that he didn't inhale, which was hardly a smooth answer, that got him into trouble. He was really quite awkward.

Does the fact that he lied about these things detract from his public character in your mind?

Yes, I think it does. And I think there's a real question of common sense involved in this. In other words, when he said, "I didn't inhale," I didn't know what the hell I was hearing. Was I hearing something that was true or false? Was I hearing somebody like a little boy saying, "Yes, I stole the cookies, but I only ate half of them?" If he had been smoother, in fact, I wouldn't have asked those questions.

The press was criticized for giving Clinton preferential treatment in '92, that negative stories were not pursued with the usual "viciousness." Do you think that's true?

Well, I don't know about viciousness, but the press pursued Gennifer Flowers and the draft business pretty hard to the point where in New Hampshire it was really make or break on those things. But remember it was up to George Bush, on the other side, to look like a candidate and he wasn't looking like a candidate. He was just looking like George Bush. And I think what happened to the press was that they felt that they only had one candidate to deal with.

When Clinton won the 1992 election many voiced a renewed sense of hope for the future of the country. In your mind, was that a genuine sense of hope, versus simply being glib rhetoric?

Yeah, I think it was genuine. I think when you take away a lot of the hardness of the clichés and the campaign, the American people, including journalists, wish the president well. And they look for a president who wishes them well.

I don't think the press looks to shoot somebody down. I think the press may turn into a shark that tasted blood, once something really bad happens, but I think most of the people in the press wish the president well. That's different from covering something up or looking the other way. They still have to tell the truth. But they are happier when the truth is happier truth.

EPILOGUE

In oral-history interviews the subject takes front stage and center. With each interview in this book, my greatest concern was to present the viewpoint of each person, his or her stances on issues, experiences and ideas, habits of thought and speech. In introducing controversial subjects, such as talk shows or journalistic bias, my intention was to point out different sides of an issue and, by and large, leave my own opinions out. But throughout the process of doing these interviews, a number of points particularly impressed me, and while they cannot be explored in depth here, they merit a brief review.

Media criticism must constantly weigh television's ability to distort against its ability to reveal. Television's sophistication is accompanied by an almost inherent anxiety about its misuse. It is so powerful, so pervasive, and sometimes so compelling, how can one not feel uneasy? Criticism of television has long been colored by fears of an ultramodern, electronic demagoguery, that television could become the ultimate vehicle for political deception and control. And rightly so. What politician wouldn't like to be the executive producer of the evening news?

Caution and rigorous criticism are appropriate, but television and television journalism also demonstrate remarkable abilities to reveal as well as distort. Television *shows* us the candidates, their faces, their hands and eyes, gestures and reactions. It's one of the oldest and perhaps most perplexing dynamics—whether it is a person sitting directly across from us or a "talking head" beamed into our living room through a satellite uplink, we are sizing up what we see and hear, looking for "the real stuff." It's a tenuous search for truth, and perhaps trust.

Watching someone on television can be so visceral and absorbing that it magnifies the ability *both* to disguise and to reveal. An old, salty truth is dredged up in greatly amplified form: what you see is not always what you get. And its attendant corollary—people can be remarkably transparent, despite their best efforts to disguise themselves.

When a candidate, day after day after day, is badgered by questions, we not only hear the candidate's words, but we see how he or she responds. Sure, Ross Perot's flipchart infommercials in 1992 were class-act exercises in political glibness. Were George Orwell alive, he would have likely watched with rapt fascination. But other televised events revealed less savory sides to Perot's character. When challenged in a debate or questioned rigorously by journalists, he didn't always appear to have all the answers. At times Perot looked testy and smallminded, outraged that he should have to defend his views to critics.

Public sophistication about what they see on television is often underestimated. The eighties saw numerous critiques of Ronald Reagan's 1980 victory over Jimmy Carter as victory of style over substance. Much of conventional wisdom had it that Republican political handlers had finally figured out how to manipulate the public through television, to trick the public into electing a former actor who was unqualified to be president of the United States. It was the beginning of the "decade of deception," the decade of the political handler. Yet even some avowed liberals now recognize that Reagan's primary power came from an ideological mandate from the public, that Reagan's beliefs and strength of character had tremendous appeal to the American public.

If Reagan had lacked what were often extraordinary communication skills, he might not have been able to form that bond with the public, but it hardly follows that he was a dummy actor following his handlers' script. No amount of masking tape on the ground or video feedback sessions could make Ronald Reagan the president he was. And this was not lost on the American public. Peggy Noonan wrote of the public's fix on Reagan—"They saw beyond the television image, they saw the flesh and blood. . . . The reporters and correspondents and smart guys, they missed it. But the public saw."[1]

Discussions of the relations between television journalists and presidential campaigns are widely framed and wisely so. Like pop culture and religion, television and television journalism are part of the chemistry of the nation's self-consciousness. Discussions of the media suffer if they are framed too tightly on the mechanics of journalism and political campaigns. The nation's ideals, the dynamics of leadership, public appetite for drama and catharsis, generational changes, and changing visual aesthetics all figure into the formula.

Critics who believed that Reagan won the 1980 election because of his slick handlers and a television-friendly personality missed the dramatic economic and social trends taking place throughout the country. People were sick of big government, sick of double-digit inflation, and sick of seeing their country humiliated abroad. And they wanted to see a certain idealism and grandeur returned to the presidency. Reagan offered that.

Did Bill Clinton win in 1992 because of his mastery of the talk-show circuit or his brilliant, brass-knuckled War Room handlers? Chances are much of Clinton's 1992 win will be chalked up to the fact that Americans had had twelve years of Reaganomics—they weren't happy and Clinton offered them a viable change.

Much of what goes on during presidential campaigns epitomizes the basic tensions between government and journalism. During presidential campaigns American journalism and politics bare their teeth on a grand scale. Our world-weariness and cynicism are great, but they are tempered by one insistent fact: the stakes are high. Presidential campaigns and their outcomes are perhaps the greatest way by which the country's course is debated and reset, through which one era ends and another begins. Americans venture into a kind of speculation which for the most part is broader than politics as usual: we think about our hopes and dreams, what we've struggled for, what kind of life we want for our children. So the journalists, the candidates, the networks, the parties, the fundraisers, handlers, pollsters, and pundits all pull out the stops.

A presidential campaign is a political Olympics of sorts, replete with debates and scandals, bludgeoning attacks, the fanfare the conventions, and the final race to the finish after Labor Day. The result is that the issues concerning journalism and politics are "writ large." If a journalist asks a particularly biting question and the candidate fails to respond effectively, its impact can be felt on an unusually wide scale. If a candidate is plagued by a tabloid story, it's not all over Louisiana or Florida or New York; *it's all over the country.*

It's as if the campaign were carried out in a vast, collective echo chamber. Particular acts and decisions reverberate for days and months afterward. The issues of journalistic responsibility, distortion, freedom of the press, the misuse of influence and power, are set in sharp relief.

The diversity of programs on television dealing with politics is a good thing. The number of so-called "New News" programs and talk shows dealing with presidential campaigns multiplied in the early 1990s. Some decried this as a further cheapening of the process. But while some programs may be weak in their practice of traditional journalistic ethics, their influence must also be measured in terms of their ability to attract and engage audiences who might not otherwise be interested in politics. Moreover, seeing candidates in multiple settings can help us get a better fix on who they are and what their views are on the issues. Town meetings, talk shows, debates, interviews, exposés, and traditional "newscasts" all offer unique vantage points for viewing candidates.

Nevertheless the diversity of programs that deal with political subjects is no excuse for irresponsibility. The fact that some journalists make a greater effort to make their coverage fair and balanced is no excuse for other journalists, interviewers, talk-show hosts, or tabloid news programs to blatantly allow unsubstantiated attacks, innuendo, and false information to go unchallenged on their broadcasts. It's a thin defense for an interviewer who knowingly allows politicians to attack their opponents without challenge to say, "Well, that's just my style. There's lots of responsible-journalism stuff out there if the audience wants that."

It's one thing to allow a candidate kindly time and emotional space to talk at length and reveal less tangible elements of his or her character. It's another to allow a

candidate to vent unsubstantiated attacks on the opposition and let them go unchallenged. To defend the latter
as an unavoidable by-product of a specific interviewing
style is about the same as saying, "Well, I have to let my
subject bludgeon his opposition with unsubstantiated
attacks, so he can feel comfortable enough to reveal his
true self."

Hard-eyed criticism counts. Some politicians and journalists privately, if not publicly, disparage media criticism
as unnecessary "handwringing" that has little relevance
to the practice of journalism or politics. There's the asser-
tion that the media is so fascinated with itself and its
power, that they feel cause to hold endless panel discussions which yield little result. And there's the "What's all
the fuss?" argument—that politics and journalism have
always been nasty, low-blow disciplines, long before the
advent of television, and that there's no evidence that it's
damaged the body politic. Finally there's the sentiment
that media critics just don't understand the limitations of
working in commercial format. But even if all of this were
true, and even if the quality of news coverage could be
proved to have minimal influence on the outcome of political campaigns, we are not at a loss for suggestions as to
how to improve news coverage. And many of these suggestions hardly threaten the commercial viability of newscasts.

Hounded by criticism after the 1988 elections that they
had fallen victim to handlers, many network news divisions assigned more correspondents to specific issues in
1992, such as the economy and health care, instead of
"on-the-bus" campaign assignments. The result was less
horse-race coverage and more coverage of issues. MTV
News's "Choose or Lose" coverage in 1992 encouraged
many young people to vote and be more informed about
issues. Much of the MTV News producers' motivation was

in response to research done by think tanks on voter turnout among young people.

Just before the 1992 presidential campaign, Kathleen Hall Jamieson, author and Dean of the Annenberg School for Communication, published a "Grammar Sheet" for news coverage of political ads based on research of how viewers absorb visual and verbal cues in television ads. The Grammar Sheet offered clear, practical guidelines for televison news "ad-watch stories." Among them were that producers frame ads in on-screen television boxes, inscribe key phrases from news reports on screen, and stamp "FALSE" or "MISLEADING" across segments which blatantly distorted the truth—all of which would increase viewers' critical distance from the ad and prevent the unfiltered rebroadcast of ads when they're covered in a news report. The ad-watch "grammar" was widely implemented. How could the networks refuse suggestions that were so concrete, so simple? How could that hurt their ratings?

One of the most important ways to improve news coverage is through the cultivation of an educated, engaged electorate. Negative ads, tabloid stories, smear campaigns, poll-driven coverage, and oversimplified rhetoric would not exist without a public appetite for them. The more engaged and knowledgeable we are, the more we will expect from news coverage and political campaigns. Journalists and politicians are, after all, consummate monitors of public opinion.

Public education, citizen forums, and TV public-service announcements are among the many effective vehicles for getting people more involved in politics and educating them about issues. Even in their ideal incarnations journalists can only hold politicians' feet to the fire so far. But as politicians and journalists well know, the public has the last word.

NOTE

1. Noonan, Peggy, *What I Saw at the Revolution* (New York: Random House, 1990), p. 151.

BIBLIOGRAPHY

Bagdikian, Ben H. *The Information Machines: Their Impact on Men and the Media.* New York: Harper & Row, 1971.

Barber, James David. *Politics by Humans: Research on American Leadership.* Durham: Duke University Press, 1988.

_____. *The Pulse of Politics: Electing Presidents in the Media Age.* New Brunswick: Transaction Publishers, 1992.

Broder, David. *Behind the Front Page: A Candid Look at How the News Is Made.* New York: Simon & Schuster, 1987.

Germond, Jack W., and Witcover, Jules. *Whose Broad Stripes and Bright Stars?* New York: Warner Books, 1989.

Goldberg, Robert, and Goldberg, Gerald Jay. *Anchors: Brokaw, Jennings, Rather, and the Evening News.* New York: Birch Lane Press, 1990.

Goldman, Peter, and Mathews, Tom. *The Quest for the Presidency 1988.* New York: Simon & Schuster/Touchstone, 1989.

Greenfield, Jeff. *The Real Campaign: How the Media Missed the Story of the 1980 Campaign.* New York: Summit Books, 1982.

Hertsgaard, Mark. *On Bended Knee: The Press and the Reagan Presidency.* New York: Farrar Straus & Giroux, 1988.

Hume, Brit. *Inside Story: Tales of Washington Scandals by the Young Reporter Who Helped Jack Anderson Dig Them Out*. New York: Doubleday, 1974.

Jamieson, Kathleen Hall. *Dirty Politics: Deception, Distraction and Democracy*. New York: Oxford University Press, 1992.

————. *Eloquence in an Electronic Age: The Transformation of Political Speechmaking*. New York: Oxford University Press, 1988.

MacNeil, Robert. *The People Machine: The Influence of Television on American Politics*. New York: Harper & Row, 1968.

Matusow, Barbara. *The Evening Stars: The Making of the Network News Anchor*. Boston: Houghton Mifflin Company, 1983.

Mickelson, Sig. *The Electric Mirror: Politics in the Age of Television*. New York: Dodd, Mead, 1972.

————. *From Whistlestop to Soundbite: Four Decades of Politics and Television*. New York: Praeger, 1989.

Noonan, Peggy. *What I Saw at the Revolution: A Political Life in the Reagan Era*. New York: Random House, 1990.

Rosenstiel, Tom. *Strange Bedfellows: How Television and the Presidential Candidates Changed American Politics*. New York: Hyperion, 1992.

White, Theodore H. *The Making of the President 1960*. New York: Atheneum, 1961.

INDEX

ABC News, 23, 25, 29; CNN's lawsuit against, 112; and cost-cutting, 33, 114; Greenfield at, 84; and MTV News, 70; reform of campaign coverage by, 85–86; Salinger at, 49, 50, 61; Shaw at, 112. *See also Nightline*

Abortion, 21, 37, 69, 79, 143, 145

Advertisements, 23, 24, 94, 88, 129; and Bush, 92, 117; elimination of, 58–59; Jamieson's Grammar Sheet for, 161; NBC coverage of, 129, 130–31; negative, 25, 59, 116, 117, 161; in the 1976 campaign, 92; and Reagan, 26–27, 92; truth of, 130, 161–62. *See also* Paid media

Afghanistan, 55–56

African-Americans, 122

AIDS, 23, 69

Alcoholism, 23, 32, 57, 80

America Held Hostage, 62, 93

Arkansas, 152

Arledge, Roone, 85

Arnett, Peter, 113

Assassinations, 4, 50, 51, 128, 148

Associated Press, 22

Atwater, Lee, 67, 68

Babitt, Bruce, 133

Baker, James, 27, 65

BBC (British Broadcasting Corporation), 4

Belfast, 143

Bentsen, Lloyd, 106

Berlin Wall, 4, 112

Bernstein, Carl, 60

Bias, xiii, 145–47, 155; and
    coverage of Reagan, 16–
    17, 52–55; and MTV
    News, 68–69, 77–78; and
    party alignments of jour-
    nalists, 11–12, 28–31, 51–
    52, 122–23
Black Monday (October,
    1987), 106
Bond, Rich, 77
Brinkley, David, 61
Brokaw, Tom, xii, 127–41
Brown, Edmund G. ("Pat"),
    128
Brown, Jerry, 73
Buckley, William, 84
Budget deficit, 25, 106, 117
Bush, Barbara, 75
Bush, George, 25, 86, 102,
    109, 154; and advertising,
    92, 117; character of, 8,
    30, 31–32, 75–77, 135,
    136; choice of Quayle, as
    a running mate, 119–20;
    debates with Clinton, 58,
    137; vs. Dukakis (1988),
    118, 119; and economic is-
    sues, 89, 90–91, 94; flag
    factory appearance, 10;
    and foreign policy, 30, 91,
    150; interview with
    Rather (1988), 5–7, 55–
    56; and the Iran–contra
    scandal, 6, 102; and *Larry
    King Live*, 35, 44, 149;
    and MTV News, 65–66,
    68, 73–74, 75–78, 80; "no

new taxes" promise made
    by, 91
Bush, Jeb, 77

California, 43, 128
Cambodia, 143
Campaigns, presidential (by
    year): *1960*, 3–4, 8–10, 49–
    50, 93–94; *1964*, 137–38;
    1968, 1, 3–4, 83–84, 94;
    1972, 93; *1976*, 43, 57, 91–
    92; *1980*, 18, 30, 84–85,
    89, 92, 157, 158; *1984*, 70,
    95–98, 101–2; *1988*, 7–8,
    26, 61, 62, 70, 84, 91, 111–
    12, 118–23, 129, 130–31,
    160; *1992*, 5, 25–26, 35,
    46, 52, 58, 62, 65–81, 85–
    88, 90–92, 94, 109, 115–
    16, 129–30, 149–51,
    153–54, 161. *See also* Con-
    ventions; Debates; Prima-
    ries; Smear campaigns
Capital punishment, 111,
    119, 143, 145, 152–53
Carter, Jimmy, 43, 57, 91–
    93, 157; character of, 47,
    138–39; and the Iranian
    hostage crisis, 29–30,
    138–39; "malaise" speech
    by, 138–39; social pro-
    grams established under,
    147
CBS News, 22, 25, 33, 53–
    56, 137; Bush-Rather in-
    terview on (1988), 5–7,
    55–56, 73; CNN's lawsuit

against, 112; and cost-cutting, 114; Greenfield at, 84
Censorship, 27. *See also* Free press
Challenger tragedy, 15, 112
Chancellor, John, 128
Character issues, xiii–xiv, 14–19, 151–54; and Carter, 47, 138–39; and Bush, 8, 30, 31–32; and Clinton, 86–88, 116–17, 131–34, 139–40, 152, 153–54; and Dukakis, 30, 111–12, 118–22; and Ferraro, 97, 99–100, 101–2, 106–8; and the primary system, structure of, 56–58; and Reagan, 15–19, 26–27, 31–32, 99, 135; and Nixon, 1–4, 37–38, 59–60, 100; and Perot, 27–28, 45–46; and talk show formats, 37–38, 39–40, 44–45, 117–18. *See also* Demagoguery; Ethics; Morality; Private lives, of candidates
China, 59, 120
CIA (Central Intelligence Agency), 120
Civil War, 12–13
Clark, Tory, 65, 66
Clinton, Bill, 25, 85–86, 91, 139–41, 150–53; campaign bus tours, 90, 94; debates with Bush, 58; and economic issues, 158; and the Gennifer Flowers story, 86–88, 116–17, 131–33, 139–40, 152, 153–54; and *Larry King Live*, 35, 38, 41, 44–45, 109; and MTV News, 67–68, 73–74, 78–81; Perot's criticism of, 45–46; populist character of, 134; and Reagan, comparison of, 18–19; and the symbolism of the presidency, 139; and talk shows, 11, 35, 38, 41, 44–45, 109
Clinton, Hillary, 87, 88
CNN (Cable News Network), 10, 35, 39, 70, 123; global scope of, 43, 112; Shaw at, 111–14; Sirulnick at, 66
Collier's, 49
Commercials. *See* Advertisements
Communism, 91. *See also* Soviet Union
Congress, 107, 147. *See also* Senate
Constitution, 100, 120
Conventions, 52, 56, 58–59, 74–75, 129, 158; CNN coverage of, 113, 115–16; Democratic, 95, 102–3, 104; Republican, 136
Cosby Show, 23
Crime, 87, 91, 111–12, 119. *See also* Capital punishment; Organized crime
Cronkite, Walter, 92–93
C-SPAN, 10
Cuban Missile Crisis, 4, 62

Cuomo, Mario, 47

Death penalty, 111, 119, 143, 145, 152–53
Death threats, xiii, 103–4
Deaver, Mike, 53–55
Debates, 24, 159; Bush-Clinton (1992), 58, 137; Bush-Dukakis (1988), 111–12, 118–23; European-style, 59; Kennedy-Nixon (1960), 3–4, 8–9, 56, 93
Decade, 69
Defense spending, 89
Demagoguery, 37, 39–40, 156
Democratic process, 10–11, 14, 37
Democratic party, 8, 52, 54–55, 60, 91, 94–95, 97–99, 111–12, 122–23, 133, 140
Dole, Bob, 41, 116–17, 135
Donahue, 44, 137
Donahue, Phil, 109, 137
Donaldson, Sam, 17, 25, 41, 108
Draft dodging, 153
Dukakis, Kitty, 111
Dukakis, Michael, xiii, 7–8, 60, 91, 106–7; and bias, 29, 122–23; character of, 30, 118–22; Shaw's question to, in 1988, 111–12, 118–23
Duke, David, 40

Economic issues, 87, 89–94, 116; and Carter, 138–39;
and Clinton's 1992 victory, 89, 158; and inflation, 92, 157; and supply-side economics, 136
Education, 11, 69, 80, 85, 86, 162
Elitism, xii, 10–11, 43–44, 86–87, 109
Ellerbee, Linda, xii, 21–34
Engle, Claire, 50
Environmental issues, 69, 80
Ethics, 109, 122, 159, 160. *See also* Morality

FBI (Federal Bureau of Investigation), 98, 103
FEC (Federal Election Commission), 98, 102–3
Ferraro, Geraldine, xii, 29, 95–109. *See also* Zacarro, John
Firing Line, 84
First Amendment, 100
Flag burning, 152
Flowers, Gennifer, 86–88, 116–17, 131–33, 139–40, 152, 153–54
Ford, Betty, 32
Ford, Gerald, 91–92, 107, 139
Foreign Affairs, 132
Foreign policy, 87, 91, 132, 152; and Bush, 30, 91, 150; Cuban Missile Crisis, 4, 62; and Ferraro, 97, 99, 106–8; and Nixon, 59; Persian Gulf War, 30, 66,

69–70, 113, 150; and Reagan, 16, 38, 89
France, 50
Freedom of Information Act, 104
Free press, 27, 159
Friedman, Paul, 85
Fund for the Conservative Majority, 102

Gandolf, Ray, 23
Garth, David, 84
Garth Associates, 84
Genovese, Tony, 103
Georgetown University, 134
Gergen, David, 43, 46, 140–41
Gingrich, Newt, 77
Goldwater, Barry, 12, 44, 137
Good Morning America, 62, 137
Goodwin, Dick, 83
Gore, Al, 35, 74
Gralnick, Jeff, 55
Great Society programs, 147
Greenfield, Jeff, xii, 83–94
Grenada, 147
Gross, Leonard, 50
Groulnick, Jeff, 85
Group W, 112
Grunwald, Mandy, 87
Gulf War, 30, 66, 69–70, 113, 150
Gumble, Bryant, 149
Gun control, 80, 145

Haig, Al, 140

Hart, Gary, 8–9, 58, 60–61, 131, 133
Health care issues, 85, 87, 132, 147
Hilter, Adolf, 27, 40
Holliman, John, 113
"Horse-race" journalism, 26, 116
Humphrey, Hubert, 43, 93, 134
Hussein, Saddam, 113

Inflation, 92, 157
Inside Politics, 113
Iowa primaries, 43, 116–17
Iran-contra scandal, 6–7, 53, 102, 107, 112, 115
Iran Hostage Crisis, 29–30, 50, 92–93, 138–39
Iran-Iraq war, 143
Iraq, 113, 143
Iraqgate, 37
Israel, 143

Jamieson, Kathleen Hall, 161
Jefferson, Thomas, 15
Jennings, Peter, 68, 85
John Paul II, 93
Johnson, Lyndon B., 51, 94, 137–38, 147
Johnson, Magic, 23
Justice Department, 102–3

Kalb, Marvin, 107
Kansas, 135
Katz, Jon, 68

Kennedy, John F., xii, xiii, 18, 78, 135–36; assassination of, 4, 50, 51, 148; character of, 57–58, 62–63; vs. Nixon (1960), 3–4, 8–9, 56, 93; and Salinger, 49, 50, 51, 53, 57–59, 62–63

Kennedy, Robert F., 49, 50, 83–84, 93, 128

King, Larry, xii, 25, 26, 35–47, 89, 94, 109, 148–49. *See also Larry King Live*

King, Martin Luther, Jr., 93

KMTV, 128

KNBC-TV, 128

Koppel, Ted, 6–7, 37, 46, 87; and Ferraro, 106–8; and Larry King, comparison of, 40–41

Larceny, 38

Larry King Live, 35–39, 62; and Bush, 35, 44, 149; and Clinton, 35, 38, 41, 44–45, 109; and the *MacNeil/Lehrer NewsHour*, comparison of, 149–51; and Perot, 35, 36, 41, 43–46, 89, 109, 137, 149, 151. *See also* King, Larry

Lebanon, 143

Legal system, 18–19, 38, 42, 108, 112

Lehrer, Jim, 3, 4–5

Lincoln, Abraham, 40, 148

Lindsay, John V., 84

Los Angeles Times, 98

Lucky Duck Productions, 21, 23

McCarthy, Joe, 39–40

McFarland, Bud, 107

McGovern, George, 50, 55

MacKinley, William, 148

MacNeil, Jane, 1, 3

MacNeil, Robert, xii, 1–19, 149–51

MacNeil/Lehrer NewsHour, 1, 4–5, 12, 13, 61, 70, 129, 143–48

Mafia, 103–4

Marijuana, 153

Matalin, Mary, 65, 77

Maxwell House, 23

Meese, Edwin, III, 103, 104

Meet the Press, 41, 107

Minnesota, 134

Mondale, Fritz, 95, 98, 105–6, 134

Morality, 99, 100, 153. *See also* Ethics

Moyers, Bill, 51

MTV News, xii, xiii, 65–81, 89, 94, 161

Mudd, Roger, 129

Murphy Brown, 98

NAFTA (North American Free Trade Agreement), 147

National Enquirer, 40, 132

National Review, 69

National Security Council, 65

NBC News, 1, 4, 5, 13, 55;
Brokaw at, 127–41;
CNN's lawsuit against,
112; cutbacks at, 114,
129; Ellerbee at, 21–23,
30–31, 32–33, 34
Nebraska, 127–28
New Hampshire primary,
72, 116–17, 154
New Jersey, 73–74
New Republic, 143, 144, 145
Newsweek, 57
New Yorker, 69
New York Times, 40
Niche marketing, 68
Nick News, 23
Nightline, xii, 29–30, 40–41,
61, 62, 93; and the Gen-
nifer Flowers story, 87–
88; and Jeff Greenfield,
83, 85, 87–88; Koppel-Fer-
raro interview on (1984),
106–7
Nixon, Patricia, 1
Nixon, Richard M., 43, 151;
character of, 1–4, 37–38,
59–60, 100; re-election of
(1972), 93, 94; vs. Ken-
nedy (1960), 3–4, 8–9, 50,
93
Noonan, Peggy, 157
NPACT (National Public Affairs Center for Televi-
sion), 3, 4

Objectivity, 12, 145–47. *See
also* Bias
O'Keefe, Constance, 98

Organized crime, 49, 97–98,
103–4
Orwell, George, 156
Our World, 23, 33
Overnight, 21, 23, 30–31

Paid media, 52, 88, 156. *See
also* Advertisements
Pan Am Flight 103 bombing,
50
Pauley, Jane, 128
PBS (Public Broadcasting
System), 3, 4–5, 129
Perot, H. Ross, 11, 25–28;
ABC special on, 86; char-
acter of, 27–28, 45–46;
and *Larry King Live*, 35,
36, 41, 43–46, 89, 109,
137, 149, 151; and MTV
News, 73, 74; and paid
media, 52, 88, 156; and
public dissatisfaction with
the political system, 88–89
Persian Gulf War, 30, 66,
69–70, 113, 150
Photo opportunities, 10, 17,
25, 52–53
Poland, 93
Pollack, Steve, 103, 104
Polling, xiii, 26, 118, 119,
123, 158, 161
Populism, 139
Povich, Maury, 25, 26
Press conferences, 11, 31–
32, 44, 60; and Ferraro,
97, 101–2; and John Ken-
nedy, 50; and Reagan, 102

Primaries: CNN coverage of, 113; Iowa, 43, 116–17; New Hampshire, 72, 116–17, 154; Super Tuesday, 117; system of, reform of, 56–59
Print media, 13, 38, 45, 56–57, 61–62, 69, 108, 123, 147, 151. *See also* Tabloids; *specific publications*
Private lives of candidates, xiii, 8–10, 99–100; coverage of, and the primary system, 56–58; and the Gary Hart episode, 8–9, 58, 60–61, 131, 133; and the Gennifer Flowers story, 86–88, 116–17, 131–33, 139–40, 152, 153–54; and John Kennedy, 57–58. *See also* Character issues

Quayle, Dan, 35, 37, 68, 78, 119–20

Racism, 69
Radio talk shows, 26, 38, 43, 78
Rather, Dan, 5–7, 55–56, 73
Ratings, xiii, 32–33, 52–53, 55–56, 108, 128, 129
Reagan, Nancy, 27
Reagan, Ronald, 29–31, 37–38, 52–55, 99, 134–35, 146, 152; and advertisements, 26–27, 92; vs. Brown, in the California gubenatorial race, 128;

Bush as heir to, 91; vs. Carter (1980), 18, 26–27, 30, 138, 156–57; character of, 15–19, 26–27, 99, 135; and Clinton, comparison of, 18–19; and the *Challenger* tragedy, 15; cutbacks under, 138, 146–47; ideological support for, 84–85, 89–90, 157; and the Iran-contra scandal, 115; meetings with the press, on helicopter pads, 17–18, 114–15; vs. Mondale (1984), 95, 98; and MTV, 67; press conferences held by, 102; shooting of, 148; and supply-side economics, 136; and the symbolism of the presidency, 15, 139, 141, 158; as the "Teflon" president, xiii, 29, 31
Religion, xiii, 107, 157
Republican party, 52, 68, 74–75, 98–99, 102–5, 111–12, 117, 122–23, 140
Reuters News Agency, 4
Rice, Donna, 133
Ripley's Believe It or Not, 33
Rollins, Ed, 46
Roosevelt, Eleanor, 47
Rosenblatt, Roger, xii, 143–54
Rutgers University, 66

Salaries, of journalists, 127, 128–29

Salinger, Pierre, xii, 9–10,
    49–63
Scherer-MacNeil Report, 4
Schlesinger, Arthur, 83
Scowcroft, Brent, 65
Senate, 49, 50, 83, 97, 103
Sexism, 69, 131
Sexuality. *See* Private lives
    of candidates
Shaw, Bernard, xii, 111–25
Show Biz Today, 66
Shultz, George, 18
Sirulnick, Dave, xii, 65–81
60 Minutes, 7, 87
Smear campaigns, xiii, 13,
    98–99, 104–5, 162
Solomon Brothers, 105–6
Soren, Tabitha, 65, 68, 70–
    71, 75–76, 80
Sound bites, 7, 61
South Dakota, 135
Soviet Union, 16, 54, 59, 62,
    150
Speechwriting, 83–84
Stephanopoulos, George, 140
Stock market crash (October
    1987), 106
"Stockholm syndrome," 28–29
Suicide, 107
Summer Sunday, 23
Superbowl, 44
Super Tuesday, 117
Supreme Court, 83

Tabloids, 40, 86–88, 132–33,
    152, 158, 159, 161
Talk shows, xiii, 25–26, 88,
    108–9, 136, 148–49, 155,

159; and character issues,
    37–38, 39–40, 44–45, 117–
    18; and Clinton, 11, 35,
    38, 41, 44–45, 109; and
    the democratic process,
    10–11; and Perot, 35, 36,
    41, 43, 44–46, 89, 109,
    137, 149, 151. *See also*
    Donahue; *Larry King
    Live*; *Nightline*; Radio
    talk shows
Taxation, 25, 89, 91, 100,
    101–2, 103, 147
Teamsters Union, 49
Terrorism, 50, 92–93. *See
    also* Iran Hostage Crisis
Terzano, Ginny, 68
Thatcher, Margaret, 106
Third-party candidates, 137.
    See also Perot, H. Ross
Threlkeld, Richard, 128
Time, 57, 143, 144, 145
Today, 128, 134, 137, 138
Town meetings, xiii, 86, 162
Trials, 18–19, 38, 42, 108,
    112
Truman, Harry S, 46
Trust, in candidates, 98,
    149, 156
Truth, 98, 105, 118, 153,
    154, 156; and advertising,
    130, 161; and the Gen-
    nifer Flowers story, 87–
    88; and skeptical
    attitudes, since Vietnam
    and Watergate, 17
Turner, Ted, 39, 112

Twentieth Century Fund, 137

Unions, 49, 113
United We Stand America, 52
USA Today, 39
USIA (United States Information Agency), 54
U.S. News and World Report, 43, 145

Vanderbilt University, 22
Vietnam, 143
Vietnam War, 12–13, 17, 60, 83, 94
Voter participation, 13, 14, 66–68, 70–71, 161

Walinsky, Adam, 83–84
Wallace, George, 43, 94, 137
Wallace, Mike, 25, 37, 41

Wall Street, Money, Greed and Power, 136
Washington Legal Foundation, 102
Washington Post, 27, 40, 144, 145
Watergate scandal, 3, 4, 17, 59–60, 92, 128, 139
WCBS-TV, 22
Weekend, 23
Week in Rock, 66
Westinghouse Broadcasting Company, 112
Woodward, Bob, 60
WorldNet, 54

Yale Law School, 83, 134
Year in Rock, 69

Zacarro, John, 29, 95–98, 101, 103–4

About the Author

LIZ CUNNINGHAM is a free-lance journalist living in the San Francisco Bay area. She is the founder of Choosing the President Forums, a non-profit educational organization dedicated to increasing participation in presidential campaigns.